FRENCH LANDING

thoughts and tribulations of a french woman moving in

ELISABETH BYKOFF

Cover Design by Christian Rafetto (www.humblebooksmedia.com)

Published in association with The Fedd Agency, Inc., a literary agency.

Fedd Books
P.O. Box 341973
Austin, TX 78734

www.thefeddagency.com

Paperback ISBN: 9781964508375

Library of Congress Control Number: 2024926975

First Edition

Printed in the United States.

DEDICATION

To all my elders who came before me and, more specifically, to my mom and dad, without whom this story would not have been possible. I hope I have made you proud.

This book is dedicated to all those who have dared to cross oceans, cultures, and continents in search of adventure, laughter, and to the brave souls who find humor in the quirks of life, and to the joy of embracing the unexpected. *Merci* for joining me on this uproarious journey from French shores to the wild wonders of the American experience.

Dear Elizabeth,
Thank you for joining me on this journey.
Keep exploring!
With gratitude,
BB

CONTENTS

INTRODUCTION

Fake It 'til You Make It

To the surprise of most people I meet, likely because I speak English with only the faintest whisper of an accent, I was actually born in Nice, France. In fact, I lived in France for the first twenty-two years of my life. By now, I've been in the United States for nearly as long—twenty years and counting. Just going by the numbers, it's been a long time since I was a fresh immigrant to this country. So, you might ask yourself, what compels me to write a memoir now? Where did the urge come from?

I guess I had nothing better to do during my lapse of employment as an executive in the startup ecosystem during the COVID era. After writing four articles on LinkedIn and attending a webinar entitled "How to Write a Non-Fiction Book Proposal," I really thought I had it in me to write a full-length book that people would want to read. Once I learned (during the aforementioned seminar) that a book proposal should be around seventy pages long, I actually believed I could pull this off without writing a proposal at all. Seriously, who would write such a tediously long document for a book barely twice the length? This is a waste of time, right? Of course, that was the primary means of securing a publishing deal, maybe even an advance on the book—but where is the fun in that? Aren't you supposed to "fake it 'til you make it"?

At least there was one thing I had going for me already: I knew how to tell a story, and I grew up wanting to tell them, just not the *written* kind. When I was still in high school, I wanted to go to the most prestigious film school in Paris, La FEMIS (Foundation Européenne pour les Métiers de l'Image et du Son). I wanted to go on to live not only in America but in an American *movie*. I wanted to have those completely unrealistic lives that they show in American movies. But I also wanted to be behind the camera. I wanted to be in film, to make movies. I was sure this desire would lead me to Hollywood, where I would get the privilege to tell audiovisual stories for very large audiences. If I followed along this path, I just *knew* that one day, my dreams would come true, and I'd get to attend the Oscars. At least that's how it worked in the mind of a naïve French teenager!

Twenty-five years later, reality looks quite a bit different from those rose-tinted dreams of my childhood. I didn't go to film school, and I am not making films. But I did make it to the United States, and I even ended up telling stories for a living. I joined a large consulting firm advising clients on their commercial operations in the tech industry and spent ten years spinning yarns for my clients every day.

Just recently, I met someone who works in the entertainment production world (movies and TV), and I shared with her my erstwhile dream of working in her industry and my current goal of writing a memoir. She advised me to endear myself to the "fake-it-'til-you-make-it" mindset if I ever did decide to make the leap into entertainment. "Most people working in entertainment know less than you or have less business experience," she'd explained. "But it doesn't stop them from getting jobs and opportunities. Find some books, learn the basics, and start pretending you're already trying to produce your own content. It's that simple. Here in LA, no one really knows what they're doing anyway."

Well, that was music to my ears because I certainly had no clue what I was doing with this book! I am *not* a writer. I've never been a writer, and I doubt I will ever be one. I never studied writing. In school, I actually hated it. If I think back to my high school days in France, I clearly recall this being one of the reasons I went into science in the first place. I wanted to follow whatever path required the fewest number of essays in order to graduate . I dreaded any type of homework or exam that involved lengthy written responses full of structure and complete sentences. Think literature, history, and philosophy. It would take me hours to get work done for those classes—too much thinking alongside my poor use of the French language. I flunked my philosophy exit exam at the end of high school and ended up with a grade of 6.5 out of 20. I still graduated from high school with flying colors, but it was not thanks to my written words. I just happened to be good at anything that involved numbers and logical reasoning. Some might say you need reason to be good at philosophy—well, in my case, that didn't work.

So here I am, writing about writing a book and all the self-doubt that comes with it. These doubts were certainly triggered during the first session with my writing coach. He gave me an assignment I needed to complete before starting to write: Read three books, understand how the authors structured their chapters, and write two chapters of my own using the same method. I did do that—if nothing else, I have always been a diligent student—and we discussed his feedback on my two chapters. I found that all his comments were valid and constructive, but to my horror, he asked me to write more: more about me, more about the other characters, and more *dialogue* . . . "Show more; don't tell!" he said. What did that even mean? How was I supposed to put more of myself out there? How was I going to write dialogue? How could I pull this off without formal training? My "fake-it-'til-you-make-it" memoir project had started to turn into an insurmountable task that I only had time to work on during weekends. Did I mention that by this time, I had secured a full-time job at a startup and was advising another one on the side, all while balancing my time with a husband and two dogs at home, managing real estate investments, taking an online film and TV essentials course, and participating in numerous other activities? It was as if I were trying to see how much I could put on my plate without breaking it. I wondered what a shrink might say about all this: *Don't you think you might have bitten off more than you could chew to avoid finishing this book?* That would be a good guess—distractions are always a good excuse for procrastination!

But in the end, I had made a commitment to myself: I would write this book and push it into the world. It might not be perfect, it might not make it onto the *New York Times* bestseller list, but I would have done it. I would have become, if not a writer, at least an author—something that, twenty-five years ago, I would have never imagined. I would have laughed out loud for even thinking about it.

Yet here I am today, sitting in front of my computer, sipping a cup of joe, and faking it 'til I make it.

And now that I'm finally ready to start writing in earnest, what am I writing about again? Oh, that's right . . .

COMING TO AMERICA

I was supposed to be born in the United States. From the start, my parents had always wanted me to have US citizenship. However, it just didn't work out that way. Originally from Gdansk known as Danzig prior to World War II, my dad, wanting to be as far from Russia as possible, left the USSR and headed west to Sweden for a job at IBM. Dad was assigned to an IBM office in France, where he met my mom, who was making money in between her worldly adventures. They started dating, eventually got married, and I was born about a year later. My place of birth was going to be Lexington, Kentucky, where my parents had friends and former American coworkers at IBM. But by the time my mom was ready to travel, her ob-gyn in France advised that the pregnancy was too far along for that plan to be a safe one. So out the door went the plan.

That is how I came to be born in Nice. I am a first-generation born and raised in France, and I consider myself quite the mix. My mom is "pied-noir," a term used to describe descendants of White French settlers in North Africa. She was born in Casablanca, Morocco, and her side of the family has origins throughout North Africa all the way to Egypt—in addition to some roots in Spain and possibly even Italy. I discovered this latest Italian fact myself through a DNA test. My mom keeps claiming the Italian genes must come from my dad's side. (Right, Mom. Are you sure we're talking about the same Dad? The one who was born in Danzig—now Gdańsk, Poland—before World War II? Whose parents were born in a country we now call Ukraine, but which back then was considered "Little Russia"?)

When my parents met, they spoke ten different languages between them but only had two in common: English and French. My dad's broken French was not his favorite, so English was the dominant language of their courtship and my early childhood. They were both working at IBM in Sophia Antipolis - La gaude, near Nice. Naturally, many of their colleagues at IBM were American expats; some of them even became close friends of our family. People often ask me why I do not have a strong French accent when speaking English. I always tell them that I got lucky. My mom told me once that, as a toddler, I used to try repeating everything I heard around me. My dad also bought me children's books in English. I was not born and raised in a typical French family, eating typical French food and reminiscing about our French heritage. We were more culturally diverse than that standard baseline. At school in France, I was known as "the American" for how well I spoke English—even better than the teacher! But I did, in fact, spend twenty-two years of my life in France. During those formative years, I had the chance to learn, embrace, and be shaped by French customs. I am French, after all!

But back to the story.

When I was six-and-a-half years old, my parents separated. I would learn the details when I was older, but about six months before my parents officially separated, my mom found a lawyer and, with the help of my grandparents, got an apartment ready for her exit. After getting all the paperwork ready, she announced it to my dad, we moved to the apartment, and they went to court. They didn't get officially divorced because the judge couldn't find any fault with either of my parents based on the evidence presented. In hindsight, it was not a big surprise or shock for me. I have memories of my parents' strained relationship and the discord having a certain effect on me during the last two years before the separation especially. I recall having psychosomatic stomach aches, which I still get from time to time when I am nervous. I remember my dad yelling or even being physical with my mom. My dad was never abusive to me. He never yelled or hit me or anything like that. I just remember the loud arguing between them. One day as I was coming down the stairs, anxious about what was happening, I ended up stumbling and rolling all the way down the stairs. I guess that is why my mom had to carefully plan her exit in secret in order to get me, my brother Matthias, and herself out. That is all she wanted, and I respect her for that. Neither my brother nor I would be the people we are today if my parents had stayed together. My dad had way too much baggage, including PTSD from World War II, that he would never admit to. He had no clue how to raise young children, and though he still loved us and would have done anything for us, I believe that if we had stayed, we all would have become dysfunctional human beings. At least, that's my guess anyway.

When I was twelve years old, my mom brought Matthias and me on a trip to the United States. It was our first time visiting this country, and we landed in Lexington, Kentucky, at the home of family friends who were my brother's godparents. The first few days felt like a whirlwind of discovering typical American tropes: Our first dinner was fried chicken from KFC (almost too on-the-nose), and our first breakfast consisted of donuts from Dunkin'.

After our stay in Lexington, we embarked on a two-week road trip from Kentucky to Washington, DC, then on to New York. It was a lot of time on the road and a *lot* of Michael Bolton music. We spent almost a week in New York, which left a major impression on my malleable twelve-year-old self. One day, while looking at the Atlas statue at Rockefeller Center, I thought to myself that I would come here again someday, and it would be for good. I just liked the vibrancy of the city. Everything felt so much bigger in New York. There was vastness all around me everywhere we went. When we got back home, I told my mom I wanted to live in the United States after high school. She agreed.

By the time my last few years of high school arrived, my mom had already started researching how to send me to college in the United States. To our mutual dismay, one day she came home and admitted to me that she simply couldn't afford it. Without family help, I knew I would have to find my way there on my own. And I did, though years later. While studying for my master's degree in aerospace engineering, I managed to get my school to restart a defunct exchange program with the University of Washington (UW). I applied, got in, and was finally on my way. It was 2004, and my first landing stateside would be in Seattle.

And that is where our story begins.

PART 1

The Early Years

CHAPTER 1

Carpet at the Airport? Really?

As part of an international exchange program, I'd been admitted into the Department of Aerospace Engineering at UW in Seattle. I left Toulouse for Paris with my mom at the end of my summer internship (I'd wrecked my car and needed a ride!). A few weeks later, I went to the US embassy to secure a visa. It was shockingly difficult to get an appointment, but that was just the first surprise in what turned out to be a long and arduous process. The embassy officials were vague about when I would get my visa, which was a bit alarming. I only had a month to get my passport back. First, I had to be on the appointment list at the entrance of the embassy. Then, I had to wait in line, literally, but we were offered seats to wait for our turn. After my first interview, I was asked to wait longer for a secondary interview (not usual). I remember thinking, *Really? I have to wait more? How long is this going to take?* First, I felt annoyed and then worried. Finally, I got a secondary interview. The US government officials had singled me out along with some of the Middle Eastern/Arabic applicants. During my interview, they asked me questions about my name, family origins, birthplace, and so on. But at some point during the meeting, they realized I was a French citizen and that my mom had been born French despite the location of her birth. No problem. Still, I had to wait to get my visa. No one could tell me when I would get it, but finally, thankfully, it arrived in time for me to fly and start school. I packed a suitcase, a big duffle bag, and a backpack. I was ready to go.

I had a boyfriend in France at the time, and as the date of my departure neared, we planned to keep up our relationship long-distance. But he didn't take me to the airport. Instead, my parents and brother took me, and we said our goodbyes there. My dad told me, "I'm proud of you, but don't you ever come back!" I was technically only supposed to be moving to America for nine months, but my visa was valid for five years—longer than the exchange program. *How am I going to use the visa for five years?* I wondered. It startled me to hear that advice from my dad. He was trying to show me that I had a rare opportunity and urged me to take it.

I boarded a Northwest Airlines flight and flew from Paris to Minneapolis—or maybe it was Detroit—where I passed through customs to board my next flight to Seattle. My layover was a little less than an hour, so I rechecked my luggage, got some snacks, and settled in to wait at my gate, exhausted but relieved to be able to sit for a moment. That's when I finally noticed the carpet in the waiting area. *Carpet? Really?*

I was jetlagged and so tired from hauling two massive suitcases and a backpack across two countries that I was afraid I'd fall asleep at the gate and miss my connecting flight. But here I was—finally on the verge of making my dream of living in America come true—and the first thing that hit me was this hideous, improbable carpet. I mean, who thought this was a good idea? What was the purpose? Was it intended to make travelers feel more comfortable? But this was an airport! Just imagine how many spills, dirty shoes, and other strange things got stuck on this carpet! And what about bugs? How clean could this carpet really even be? How often was it cleaned? Carpet was not standard flooring at any European airports, and at that moment, I couldn't recall noticing the carpet during my previous trips to the United States. *How can such an entrepreneurial and advanced country do this?* I wondered. *What are they thinking?* I couldn't let it go. I started to panic. *Should I be worried? What if I don't fit in here?*

On that Tuesday evening, overwhelmed, excited, and exhausted all at once, I found that my fears finally surfaced, and they latched onto the first thing they could find, which was apparently the carpet. I had wanted this move so badly that I never really stopped to consider what it would mean, nor had I thought about the potential difficulties or obstacles I might face in my new home. *I mean, how different could it be?* I had been full of hope and high on unrealistic expectations. But now that I was finally on American soil—well, American *carpet*—I was beginning to understand that my "American dream" was going to look much different in reality than it had in my idealistic imagination.

CHAPTER 2

What Did You Learn at School?

As a visiting graduate student at UW in the Department of Aerospace and Aeronautics, I was required to enroll in a few prerequisites—400-level classes—in addition to my regular 500- and 600-level courses to complete my degree. I didn't think much of the requirement and dutifully signed up for the 400-level courses I needed to graduate. Now fully registered, I was ready to go.

I still remember that first 400-level class. I sat down, opened my brand-new notebook, and waited eagerly for my very first class in the United States to start. Then came the shock: The professor started his lecture by saying, "Today, we are going to learn all about matrices." Matrices? I thought, with a puzzled look on my face. But I had to master those in high school in order to graduate. Hadn't the rest of the students in this course learned these in high school? What was I missing? Apparently, a lot. Or rather, my classmates were. I had taken for granted that the math skills I'd learned in high school represented some kind of international standard, but, as I was now learning, I'd been wrong about that. It was clear that my American classmates had not experienced the same kind of math curriculum I'd had back home—at least, not enough of them for the university to consider a lesson on matrices unnecessary for students pursuing engineering degrees.

Much like my experience with the airport carpets, I was feeling culture shock in my 400-level courses. In an attempt to understand this strange new academic environment, during my time out of class, I started researching the overall school system in the United States in an effort to compare it to the one I'd been raised in. I quickly realized the differences were vast with respect to both culture and infrastructure. Here are the main differences I noted for your entertainment:

1. FRANCE IS A CENTRALIZED COUNTRY.

Unlike the United States, the education system in France is centralized, meaning that all schools, including private schools, must follow the same core curriculum. There are no charter schools. Private schools can require religious studies classes on top of the base curriculum, but everyone takes the same exams to graduate, no matter what kind of school they attend.

Learning a second language is mandatory as part of this universal curriculum, starting in middle school. In the sixth grade, each student picks a first non-French language (usually English or German). Eighth graders have to start taking a third language. Studying a minimum of two foreign languages is required until graduation, with the option of adding a third language in high school.

Education is one of the biggest line items in France's budget, second only to military spending. The emphasis on education is even more pronounced because the French government is built on a unitary system, meaning the national government has ultimate authority, not the provinces. This is in direct contrast to the way the US government works, where the federal government shares power with the states, which often leads to big differences in budgeting priorities from state to state. Depending on where my new American classmates had attended high school, their states may have allocated more spending to STEM classes or football programs.

With respect to my own education, engineering school in France was not part of my university degree (it is for some, but I took a different path). There, if you want an engineering degree, first you attend prep school for your basic classes, then the specialized schools in your field of study. French students can take classes in engineering at university, but not as an entire focus the way undergraduate students do in the United States. As a result, it took an extra year for me to get into the school I wanted. (That's what happens when you entertain your brother's godmother and relatives from America instead of studying for the oral exam!)

2. ALL FRENCH CHILDREN BEGIN SCHOOL AT AGE THREE.

The "La Maternelle" mandate, passed in 2019, requires that all French children begin school at age three, but I can tell you that even prior to the mandate, most parents in France were already in the habit of enrolling their children in preschool so they could get back to work. If you are a January baby, like me, you get to start school at two-and-a-half years old. Nice! Children attend preschool five days a week for a total of twenty-four hours of learning. I was surprised to learn that, depending on the state my American classmates had grown up in, school was only mandatory starting at age six—in some states, as late as eight years old!

In France, when I was growing up, a typical week of preschool looked like this: Full days of school on Monday, Tuesday, Thursday, and Friday, plus a half-day on Saturday. Wednesday was off. Since then, the program has changed, so Wednesday is now a half-day, and both Saturday and Sunday are off. Twenty-four hours of learning per week meant we would start class at 8:30 a.m. and end each day at 4:30 p.m., with one recess break in the morning, one recess break in the afternoon, and a long lunch break (we are still French, after all). That meant we were actually spending thirty-six hours per week at school. School is essentially a full-time job for French kids starting at age three. This both allows their parents to work and provides socialization starting at a very young age.

3. IN FRANCE, HIGH SCHOOL IS SIX DAYS A WEEK.

Attending school five times a week continues throughout elementary school and into "college" (middle school in the United States). Then, when students get to high school, attendance shifts to six days a week. There are four full days of classes on Monday, Tuesday, Thursday, and Friday and two half-days on Wednesday and Saturday. French students now have around thirty-six hours of learning, so recess and lunch breaks become shorter. Students' only job at that point in life is learning. The government-determined slate of main classes is mandatory: French, math, history, geography, science, English, a second foreign language, etc. In addition, students get to select optional classes every year, such as another foreign language, Greek or Latin, liberal arts, technologies, and so on. The goal of this sometimes-tedious process is to ensure French students graduate as well-rounded individuals with a shared baseline amount of knowledge about the rest of the world.

After my rigorous experience of education as a full-time job back in France, the relative laxity of my American university courses was initially quite a shock. But in the end, it was also helpful because the easy classes allowed me to focus more of my energy on improving my English language skills. Aside from my new classmates, I got the most practice speaking English with the friends of friends who hosted me when I moved to the United States while I was still looking for my own housing. I had about one week of their hospitality before I had to find another place to live, so I'd already scouted out some places via the now-less-popular Craigslist while I was still living in France. By this time it was 2004, but I still had no cell phone and had to make all my calls to prospective rentals from a pay phone. Finally, I found a room to rent in a house with five roommates—all guys. The rooms were unfurnished, so I found myself back on Craigslist, where I sourced a desk and chair for myself. I didn't have a car and lived about a mile or so west of campus, so I took a bus to class every day for the three years I attended UW.

To my delight, UW had a good international community, and the FIUTS program I attended offered a lot of assistance to international students trying to acclimate. Overall, though, I avoided the other French students so I could focus on improving my English.

All in all, that first year of coming to the United States ended up being a softer landing than expected when it came to education and finding a place to live. The French education system had given me a small leg up on the class work and I could focus mainly on writing my thesis. And by avoiding my fellow citizens, I was able to beef up my English and start my real assimilation into the American culture of my heavily-influenced-by-movies dreams.

CHAPTER 3

The Credit Score Plot

A few months after landing in the United States, I'd been accept-ed into UW's MBA program and was now sure I would be stay-ing for longer than the original nine months. I decided it was time to get a cell phone so I could be reached more easily by my loved ones and new friends. I also had a new American boyfriend, and I want-ed to be sure I could reach him at any time. (I'd broken up with my long-distance boyfriend back in France by this time.)

Just like everyone else in search of something in America, I made my way to the mall. Remember, this was way back in the early aughts! The iPhone still had not come out and smartphones didn't quite exist yet, so I proceeded to the AT&T store—where my boyfriend had his cell phone plan—for a new, non-smartphone. I browsed through my options at the store before starting the process of securing a plan. Almost immediately, the store employee assisting me asked for my Social Security number. My *what*? The number for health expense reimbursement? No, wait, that wasn't right. "Social security" in France is the equivalent of national healthcare insurance and not tied to individual credit or taxes. I apologized and explained I didn't have a Social Security number. The employee started to ask questions about my credit history and my credit score. Excuse me, my *what again*? I was told I could not secure a phone or a plan without a credit history, and if I wanted to obtain a phone plan, I'd need to find a cosigner with some kind of credit history. I was twenty-two, and I needed the equivalent of a parent to secure a cell phone. *What on earth?*

Everything about this experience made no sense to me. Wasn't it a good thing not to have a credit history, meaning I hadn't borrowed money or missed any creditor payments? No, ma'am. Here in the United States, it seemed that the more money you borrowed, the better. But why? Who thought this was a good idea? Back in 2005, France didn't have a very developed credit landscape. What we called "credit cards" in France were more akin to debit cards with costly overdraft options. And, to be honest, my parents and grandparents would never have taught me to buy anything on credit anyway. Why would you do that? Wasn't it better, financially, to buy within your needs and never overextend yourself? To save as much as you could instead of spending beyond your means?

To this day, I still struggle with the concept of credit and a credit score. It seems as if the entire plot is to push people to spend more than they should in the hopes that they will default on their debt and get charged atrocious interest rates. This credit score determines how much you can borrow for big purchases like a car or a home, but you can barely figure out how it is calculated. And if you haven't built up a credit history since you were born, good luck with your future. I have heard of parents opening credit card accounts in their kids' names at an early age just so they can start building up their credit history. What a gift! "Let me build some debt history for you so you're better positioned to borrow more later in life at a more advantageous rate." What a trip!

Dismayed by my experience at the AT&T store, I went home, scratching my head over how I was going to secure a cell phone. Who would vouch for me and be my cosigner? Not knowing who else to turn to, I decided to ask my boyfriend, who already had an AT&T plan of his own, after all. To my relief, he didn't flinch at all and said, "Sure. Why not?" I assured him he wouldn't regret this, as I would pay for everything myself—I just needed his credit. We took another trip to the store, and he helped me open my first US cell phone line with AT&T. I am still with them more than fifteen years later. The funny part is, in the end, I had to secure a Social Security number and open my first credit card with Bank of America only a few months later. By then, I had forgotten that my then-boyfriend had been a cosigner on my original phone plan, so he ended up being on that plan for years until I finally requested for him to be dropped—long after we had split. Nonetheless, I can still thank him for that very first cell phone!

Back to that very American concept of credit and credit scores, I always wondered why people felt compelled to create or promote financial literacy programs in schools—as if young minds needed to be taught about money! But I get it now. This entire system feels like it was built to mainly screw people over. Please borrow more than you can afford, get into debt, and good luck getting out of it. No wonder people are trying to teach kids not to get into financial trouble. What do you think? It's so challenging to navigate credit cards, mortgages, lines of credit, loans, and more. And then add to that the sophistication of investing in the public markets, even just for your retirement, and there you have it, folks—an entire system based on the idea that you need money to make money. Your score dictates your entire financial health and future prospects. Isn't it a bit discriminatory? Think about it: One score influences your ability to rent, buy a house, a car, a phone, or even insurance. These are the foundations of life in America—housing, transportation, and communication (especially in this age of mobile phones). Just add food and healthcare and it encompasses everything a person needs to live securely. I get why credit scores can be useful—why would we keep lending to people who can't repay their debt? Well, maybe let's not let them get into debt in the first place with all those store credit cards calling our names. What a thought, right? I am not sure I have an answer to this quite large problem, and some of those credit instruments are being made available and becoming popular back home in France. Can you imagine a French credit score? People would get all up in arms and call it BS. But if our scores were based on our culinary prowess, our wine and cheese, our pastries, and our fashion, we might be fine!

CHAPTER 4

Dating Means Learning to Hedge Your Bets

When I first arrived in this new country, one of the things I was most intrigued about and afraid of was the prospect of dating. Keep in mind that when I landed in the United States, I was still with my French boyfriend of three years. We'd agreed to stay together long-distance before I left, assuming I would be home in nine months, and we would resume our lives together. Since I've been here for about twenty years now, you can imagine that those plans changed. About a month into this arrangement, making early morning or late-night calls back to France, we decided it would be better to go our separate ways. It was heartbreaking, but we knew it was the right thing to do. After all, we had been dating on and off before I came to America and had been slowly drifting apart. We'd just got back together before I left. It didn't help that I had no plans to come back to France before those initial nine months were up, and he had no plans to visit me in the United States. To make matters more challenging, I was roommates with five guys around this time, and one had begun flirting with me . . .

Here I was, twenty-two years old in a foreign land, wondering what this dating thing was all about. During my first three years, I wouldn't say that I had the typical American dating experience. I quickly fell for one of my roommates—and fell *hard*—and he broke my heart.

The relationship didn't really have a usual start—we were already living together. Our courtship had taken place within the house, hanging out with our roommates or other friends. There was no tedious scheduling to work out in order to see each other and plan dates. Our first dates were already going out with each other's friends and meeting his family. About a month in, we were already taking a trip to East Washington to attend the Apple Cup. Two months of dating and he was helping me with my UW MBA application, specifically helping edit my essay. Three months in, we spent my birthday weekend in Chicago, as he had planned to attend a training there the following week. So, there we were in snowy Chicago, checking out all the first-time tourist spots, eating deep-dish pizza, and all in all having a great time. I remember thinking it was going so fast, but I was sinking into the idea that I had found *the one*. What made me so sure? When your subconscious decides to show you a dream one night where you're having a kid together, I think that says it all. I felt I'd found my Prince Charming and was living a significant part of my American dream.

You can imagine how I felt when, after getting home on my own, I was not able to reach him the following night. My brain went into overdrive. I had to call him on his cell from my landline (I still had no cell phone) and needed to be home for him to call me back, which didn't happen until the next evening. Despite my suspicions, I didn't linger on it, and he came home later that week like nothing had happened. But over the next few weeks, his behavior changed toward me—especially compared to the weekend we spent in Chicago. Eventually, I confronted him, asking him what had changed, and he admitted that he had slept with someone in Chicago. He said, "Yes, a day or two after you left, and we had such an amazing time." After that, I was stupid enough to think I could stay at the house and that it would be just fine. I guess I was naïve, or maybe we lived in two different realities, but in any case, the next four or five months were painful. I was so heartbroken that I couldn't even eat. All my sadness and frustration ended up in my belly. In addition to learning that he'd cheated on me, I also learned that he had done it without protection and came home not thinking about the consequences. I had to fight for him to finally agree to get tested along with me. Who does that? If you are going to cheat on someone, at least use protection. He didn't even know this woman for five minutes. No need to bring any undesirable present home. And what about your own health? How careless can you be?

After this debacle, my mom visited from France, and then he started to act like a boyfriend again, on his best behavior. He offered to pick her up at the airport and take us for dinner when she first landed. It was the weirdest thing ever. They ended up talking about me as if I was not there. Trading stories, laughing, and enjoying each other's company. I remember telling my mom, "What the hell?" and she responded, "What did you expect me to do? I can't just be an ass to him. I just went with the flow." Thanks, Mom! With this and a few other unexpected incidents, like kissing me goodbye one night, we ended up back together a few months after the initial break up. And that was the worst part. I was pretending the cheating didn't affect me, but the fear of him cheating again was pretty much constant. Every time he would go out alone with friends, especially at night, I'd wake up, wait for him to come home and for the axe to fall again. All the while writing my thesis, going out with my friends, and getting ready for my MBA, I had this cloud over my head, thinking this relationship could be salvaged. The school year ended and I had to go back to France to present my thesis and graduate before coming back for my MBA. All the roommates were going their separate ways, some were returning to Europe, some were moving away or moving in with other people—so I did the same. I found another house a block away full of UW students who were looking for another roommate, and I moved there when I got back from France. That was the end of year one in the United States. It was the end of the house of quirky roommates and the end of my relationship with him. We didn't really stay in touch, but we would exchange the odd text for birthdays and holidays. All in all, I had to grieve the relationship and bring myself back to reality. I was not going to find *the one* in the first American I dated. How lucky would that have been!

Once I was over my heartbreak, I spent some time meeting a few guys, but none of it was serious, just flirtatious, short-lived relationships. A few years later, after I got my MBA, I moved from Seattle to San Francisco to start my career as a consultant at a Big Four firm. That's when I decided to really put myself out there and try this thing called "dating."

The concept of dating in the United States was foreign to me, and I had to learn a completely different set of rules for this game. Let me tell you, in France, there is no equivalent to "dating." If we like someone, we go all-in from the start and focus on one person at a time. If the relationship doesn't work out, it's no big deal. We just move on to the next one with no hard feelings (*most* of the time—of course, sometimes one side might be much more disappointed than the other). In the United States, my new American friends explained to me their idea of dating.

From what they told me and my own experiences, here are the "rules" I've gathered:

1. **Play hard to get.** Even if you are interested, pretend you are not . . . Men love the chase!

2. **Don't be yourself.** Put on a show of being a nicer person than you really are. Basically, become someone else.

3. **Date multiple people at the same time.** Keep your options open in case a few don't work out.

4. **Don't be exclusive right away.** No one commits to exclusivity on their first few dates. Just keep fooling around with all of them.

5. **Keep your eyes out for better options.** You never know, someone better might be right around the corner!

When I think about all these rules taken together, they're not that bad. But a couple of practical concerns do come to mind:

- How "hard to get" should I be playing? Where do I draw the line between enticing someone to chase me and turning them off?

- What kind of persona should I create? Do I have to create a different one for each date? Should I base that persona on what I think my date might like? How do I even keep track of all these personas?

- Logistically, how do I even keep track of all these people I'm meant to be dating at the same time? How do I keep straight in my head who they are, what they like, and what I've already told them? How much time do I have in one week to spare for all these dates? Come on! Dating one person is already a *lot* of work, especially when I take into consideration the time spent thinking about whether I even like him or not, whether he is going to call, or what I'm going to text him next. It's exciting, sure, but also time-consuming! Most of us have jobs to focus on!

- Am I supposed to just start sleeping with several men at the same time and feel safe? Of course, protected sex is essential (even though I could write an entire chapter on American men refusing to use condoms, but I will save that for another book) but doesn't increasing your number of sexual partners also increase your risk of catching a sexually transmitted infection, regardless of how careful you're being? Seriously.

To this day, I still don't really get the rules, and I can tell you I was never good at dating by American standards. I never really wanted to date several men at the same time, so I didn't hedge my bets by juggling suitors. And I was never really able to play hard to get or pretend to be someone else. To be honest, I never really allowed men to hassle me at bars, clubs, and other places. I was told I was intimidating, which I'm sure closed the doors on a lot of possibilities. Do I feel regretful about it? Absolutely not. Might I have missed some interesting opportunities? I am sure I did. Some of you might be saying to yourselves, "Oh girl, what were you thinking?" Obviously, I *wasn't* thinking, but I believe it turned out quite fine for me. My husband and I have been together for more than ten years now, even though I broke all possible rules with that relationship. And it turned out okay! But again, maybe his English background might have played a role . . . I didn't try to catch an American guy. I guess I just took the European route, after all. Who would have thought?!

CHAPTER 5

Driving—What a Joke!

The year I graduated from the UW MBA program, about three years after landing in the United States, my mom visited to attend my graduation, and she was very excited about shopping. I thought it would be a good idea to take her to the outlets not too far from Seattle. Since I didn't own a car, one of my roommates at the time agreed to lend us his car, a massive Chevrolet Impala. I didn't have an American driver's license at the time and was still using the international driver's license I'd secured back in France for my stay in the United States. Just imagine two French ladies on the smaller side (my mom is 5'2", and I am 5'5") maneuvering this oversized car. Anyway, we planned the route and printed the directions (still no smartphone), and off we went. My mom was chatting with me the entire time, I lost track of speed limits, and of course, the inevitable happened. We got stopped by Washington State Patrol. Here we were, in the middle of the highway, stopped, and the officer came around to my window asking for my license and registration. At this point, I was freaking out: If there is one thing you get taught in France about the United States, it's "Do not mess up with the law and don't get arrested." So, I was praying to the driving gods that I would get out of this mess with a ticket.

The officer started asking me questions, and my mom felt it would be helpful if she leaned over and innocently told the officer that it was her fault, as she was chatting me up and distracting me. He didn't take it kindly, just shrugged, and I ended up with a reprimand and a ticket. He literally had to write it up on a lovely pink slip, and since I did not have a driver's license, he could only fine me—no threat of points against my license. As we continued our journey to the mall, I regained my composure and we reached our destination, the outlet. Apparently, this incident didn't faze my mom at all, as she ended up buying exactly what she was looking for and more. For me, the memory remained as an experience I really didn't enjoy. I was scared, my heart rate was up, and I ended up getting cold sweats. It took me a little while to calm down and wash out the anxiety. I have been stopped, warned, and ticketed a couple more times since then, and I still dread those stops. Somehow, maybe through watching too many American movies when I was a kid and getting told not to mess around with the law for fear of getting thrown out of the country, any encounter with the law is one of the few American "traumas" that has stayed with me.

So given the consequences of breaking the rules of the road, it has always been puzzling to me to see sixteen-year-olds behind the wheel in the United States. They seem so young! Don't get me wrong: in France, you can secure a permit starting at sixteen, but you have to endure two full, painful years of driving with one of your parents until the magic moment when, at the age of eighteen, you pass your driving test successfully.

Here's how the process of acquiring a driver's license goes in France:

- As you get closer to your sixteenth birthday, you enroll in a driving school. You then have to go through your mandatory twenty hours of driving with a certified instructor, who teaches you everything from driving in town to highway driving to parking properly (especially parallel parking!).

- At the same time, you attend a driving school studying "Le Code de la Route," which is a road rule book. You have to take a quite difficult written test before you can even be considered for the driving test. The rule book is quite extensive. It feels like there are way more road rules in France than in the United States and that you must learn all the potential combinations. The test doesn't fit on a slip—it is forty questions taken from a bank of over a thousand questions, and you have to answer thirty-five of those correctly in order to pass. The questions vary from multiple-choice to scenarios where you're shown a video, sometimes requiring answers not from the driver's perspective but from that of a pedestrian or another driver.

- Assuming you pass the test and complete your twenty hours of driving education, you are issued a permit at the age of sixteen. You then have the pleasure of spending quality time with your parents, who are nervous and freaking out about the good (most likely bad) driving habits you are acquiring, with them sitting next to you for the next two years.

- When you turn eighteen, it is time for you to take the dreaded driving test. Keep in mind this doesn't happen in your own car but in a state-sponsored car with three other candidates and the instructor present. Each of us gets to drive the car for fifteen minutes, including a parking try. This is the last opportunity you have to unlearn all the bad habits you picked up in the last two years with your parents and try to remember all the good things you learned with your instructor two years ago. For this reason, most driving schools offer a one-hour refresher course before the exam to ensure you don't forget to turn on your blinker, look into your blind spot before switching lanes, practice parallel parking, and come to a complete stop at the stop sign!

- The driving test usually occurs in a city close to your home but also somewhere that you, most likely, haven't spent a lot of time. Then you have the opportunity to succeed or fail in front of strangers . . . no nervousness at all!

- Congratulations, you passed! (Maybe.) You are now eighteen—legally an adult in France—and you can drive a car on your own. If you fail your test, they recommend taking another hour of driving at your driving school and then booking your test again based on availability. You do not have to take the written test again. If you pass that one, it is for life.

My understanding of the process of obtaining a driver's license in the United States is that it depends on the state you live in:

- At fifteen, you can secure a learner's permit. In some states, you have to take some driving classes before applying for one. In most states, you can study for a written exam at home using your state's own rules of the road book. Then, you show up to the Department of Motor Vehicles, the Department of Public Safety, or whichever transportation agency handles licensing in your state at your scheduled appointment time. In some areas, you can even take the written-only test during a walk-in appointment!

- During your appointment, you fill out some forms, take an eye test to determine that your vision qualifies you to drive, and take a written-only test. The test has multiple-choice questions and is graded on the spot by an employee. If you pass, you get a permit, which allows you to operate a vehicle as long as a fully licensed driver is in the car with you.

- In the year before you turn sixteen, you must log between thirty and fifty hours of driving with a licensed driver, depending on the state. This person can be a qualified driving instructor, your parents, or even an older brother or sister.

- When you turn sixteen, you can schedule an appointment for a road test. If you can produce written confirmation that you've completed the required driving hours with a licensed driver, then you can begin the test. The road test is fifteen minutes long and takes place in town, with no freeway driving requirement. Depending on the

state, you might not need to demonstrate any parking
abilities, either!

- If you pass the road test, you are all set with a few restrictions, which vary by state but usually include passenger limits and curfews. Some states have no restrictions for minor drivers, and their licenses are essentially the same as those held by adult drivers.

When I eventually moved to San Francisco, I had to go through California's (adult) version of this process, which I found to be shockingly easy. I booked the appointment at the DMV, took the written test after barely reading the little book provided online, and passed. They performed my eye check, and then I had to wait for the road test. I had to provide my own car (it was my roommate's), which the instructor got into, and then we were off. It was barely a ten-minute drive in the hills of San Francisco. We stopped at a few stop signs, made some right and left turns, and made one parking attempt, and that was it. There was no highway, no parallel parking; it was easy-peasy. The instructor even told me, "Be careful not to do rolling stops, even on a hill." And that was all it took to get my driver's license in the United States!

I think that, in many cases, the nature of this brief learning process means that Americans have not been taught how to properly drive in town, on the highway, or how to park. And it is quite telling when you drive on US highways, depending on the state: The left lane can get packed with all the traffic while the right lane is wide open. Or in town, you watch US drivers trying to parallel park and it takes them quite a few tries.

We have quite a different driving style back home. In a way, they teach us more than just driving; they also teach us proper driving etiquette. And you can get fined if you do not follow it. It is the law, after all. Driving in town is almost an art. We have way smaller streets (smaller cars, too), but you have to learn to navigate space as well as traffic. My favorite thing to do when I was driving back in France was to take the Arc de Triomphe roundabout. It is lawless when it comes to driving. You've got to commit, or you will never get through it. The thrill, the speed, and the excitement—I even miss it. Negotiating the cars to get ahead and taking the exit you want, I never experienced anything like it in the United States.

On the highways, the proper etiquette is to drive in the right lane and use the middle or left lane to pass slower traffic. As soon as you have passed one or several vehicles, it is customary to get back in the right lane. If you do not, people will flash their lights and let you know about it. And you can even get stopped and ticketed by the police if they catch you. No joke! But it makes for a much safer highway experience and way less traffic. At no time will you ever get stuck between three cars, one in each lane, all driving exactly at the same speed and blocking traffic. It's infuriating! Parking, of course, is the holy grail of driving skills. I always joke about it. If you can parallel park, you can park anywhere. Remember, they test us on parallel parking during the license test in France. Also, parallel parking is most of the parking you encounter throughout France. We have nothing like the sheer number or size of parking lots here in the United States. So, you'd better learn it and learn it fast, because you need it and you do not want to be made fun of by your family and friends. It's a bit like a badge of honor. Funny enough, more recently, a friend of mine was driving, and we found the perfect parking spot in front of the restaurant. I offered to park her car as it required parallel parking, and I knew for a fact she couldn't do it. She politely declined, went around the block, and parked at the back of the restaurant in their parking lot.

At sixteen, you are in high school. You are insouciant and enjoying life. You can be daydreaming, absent-minded, and just learning about what life is all about. You hang out with friends; you go to parties and build relationships that might last a lifetime. Is it a little early to provide that kind of responsibility to a teenager? This is the time they start thinking about what they want to do when they grow up. Shouldn't they be focused on that instead of being allowed to operate a piece of machinery that can bring death if not operated properly?

You might be thinking, *Who the heck does she think she is? This is quite a judgmental chapter!* And I would not challenge you on that. I was desperate to get my license back in France because I just wanted to finally be independent from my parents. I wanted to have the freedom to do whatever and go wherever I pleased. But thinking back to who I was at sixteen, I realize now that I thought I was on top of the world and that everything was open to me. I think I would have taken too many risks, believing nothing could happen to me. I could have potentially gotten myself into a lot of trouble. And then what? Despite the annoyance of having to wait, it did teach me patience.

The two years in and of themselves really taught me patience. I had to go through the process and clock those kilometers to complete this permit and take my driver's license test. No shortcuts, no workarounds, and my mom always refused to let me get a moped or Vespa like some of my friends. So, it was all public transportation for me or driving with my mom in the passenger seat. Through those two years, you gain experience, confidence, and an understanding that when you're sitting behind the wheel, you are responsible for whatever happens. A car is not a toy, and it can be dangerous for you and others. And your parents are always happy to remind you of that even when you make a small mistake while driving with them. I still couldn't wait to complete the process, get my license, and finally be independent. Somehow, I saw securing my driver's license as a big piece in gaining my independence and graduating into adult life.

I really do not want to die behind the wheel. No, thank you!

CHAPTER 6

The Art of the Doggy Bag

As I mentioned earlier, my first encounter with American food was during our first visit to the United States in 1994, and it was nothing short of iconic. My mom, brother, and twelve-year-old me were staying with family friends in Lexington, Kentucky, and after our host picked us up at the Cincinnati airport, we stopped to pick up dinner at . . . Kentucky Fried Chicken! A full bucket of it! What an apt first American dinner in Kentucky!

The first thing that caught my eye about that classic American meal was the sheer amount of chicken and sides our host ordered for the five of us. Shortly after that observation, I had my first experience of the deliciousness of fast-food fried chicken, the sweetness of coleslaw, and the starchy mashed potatoes and gravy. How many calories could you pack in one dinner? But that wasn't the end of it. The next morning, I was introduced to what would become my second-favorite guilty pleasure (the first, ironically, being French fries;

I can't help myself!) . . . Dunkin' Donuts. With the aim of introducing us to "real" American food, our host took us to Dunkin' for a dozen. Big mistake! That first week in the United States turned into a breakfast-feeding frenzy for me. Can you justify a twelve-year-old French girl eating five donuts a day for almost seven days straight? I hope not. I don't really know how I survived that experience. All I know is that I decided if buying a dozen donuts was cheaper than half a dozen, I was all in!

If polishing off half a box of donuts every day for a week had been my only experience of American food's enormous portions, then it honestly wouldn't have been that bad. But, of course, it didn't stop there. As we made our way around Kentucky and visited other restaurants in the area, I discovered a few other things about food in America.

Here, there was no need for a three-course meal. One entrée was more than sufficient. While back home, we'd been accustomed to ordering an appetizer, an entrée, and a dessert—finished off with an espresso at the end of the meal—it was impossible to do the same in Kentucky. We made that mistake at one of the first restaurants we stopped at, and by the time the entrée showed up, we were already full. The appetizers could have fed most of us for a couple of meals, honestly. I was left wondering how most Americans could pull off eating three dishes when the portions were that gigantic. Maybe French portions were exaggeratedly small? This is a criticism you sometimes hear from tourists coming to France from other countries. To be fair, how do French restaurants justify such expensive food when portion sizes are maybe three to four times smaller than they are in the United States?

But the differences between the French and American dining experience didn't stop there. At the beginning of dinner, we kids were asked what we wanted to drink. Without hesitation, we asked for "cokes"—a generic term for any soft drink in the American South, called "soda" or "pop" in other parts of the United States. Being good French kids, we paced ourselves with our drinks, trying to make them last for the whole meal. However, we discovered that, with the amount of food we were served, we drained our glasses much faster than we'd expected. Without hesitation, the waitress came over and asked if we wanted "refills." We looked at our hosts with puzzlement and asked, "What are refills?" They explained that in most restaurants, you could get an unlimited amount of coke when you buy one glass. We were astounded. I could have infinite cokes throughout dinner without paying an extra penny. What a deal! But was it really necessary? I could barely eat my whole dinner, and now I also had the option of drinking myself to death, too? Where did the amount of food and beverages end? Were all meals this way? How would I learn to pace myself? Is this why the doggy bag was invented? This was a concept that didn't exist in France either. No one would ever dare to ask for a doggy bag to bring leftovers home. It would be quite offensive.

The funniest part was that after we were made aware of this abundance of food, we realized that at fast-food and sit-down restaurants, portions were clearly oversized for any regular person. Did you ever order a "supersized" Coke at McDonald's in the '90s? No one in their right mind could have finished off such a large beverage, especially when you added in a Big Mac and a large fry. Or *could* they? I was equally baffled by all-you-can-eat menu items at chain restaurants such as the Olive Garden. I love pasta, but how many servings can you seriously eat in one sitting?

I was extremely worried I would put on weight. "The memory of the enormous portion sizes and endless refills was defintiely fuel to the fire. A friend of mine from France was moving with me, and I decided we would make a pact not to overdo it together, and we didn't. As students, we ended up making carefully portioned food for ourselves at home, ensuring we would not cave and eat fast food every day. But it was hard. With the pressure of not having a lot of money, it became really appealing to just buy a cheap oversized meal and try to save the extra for the next day. Okay, who are we kidding? No one would ever save extra fries or Coke for the next day.

Twenty years into living in the United States, I am still amazed by American portion sizes. But surprisingly, I've also become annoyed with small French portions. It's almost a contradiction between how I was raised and my adopted country. As a child, my parents and grandparents would always expect me to finish what was on my plate. Our portions, whether at home or at restaurants, had always been quite manageable for a child, and adults were adept at making us kids feel guilty, reminding us that there were kids in Africa dying of hunger, and therefore, there was no reason to waste or throw away any food. So, when I got to the United States and experienced all the generous portions of food you get with every order, I felt almost obligated to finish my plate. Good luck with that if you ever end up at Olive Garden or any of the other chain restaurants, or any of the non-fine-dining establishments, honestly. You know what I mean. So, I moderated myself, but I got used to the amount of food and the price I paid for it in America. Over the years, my expectations changed, and I have learned the art of the doggy bag, using it to ensure I don't always finish what is on my plate and save the rest for later. What a sweet deal and something you will obviously not find in France. Sacrilege! I think I get it now! Or do I? When I go back home to France these days, I am disappointed with the price I have to pay for the amount of food I get. How did I ever think it was okay to pay so much for such a small amount of food? My frame of reference has obviously evolved, but have I overcorrected? Is there a middle ground between quality and quantity? What if I could eat two croissants for the price of one? Or even better, what if the French *pain au chocolat* were sold by the dozen like at Krispy Kreme? Any takers?

PART 2

Career and Financial Independence

CHAPTER 7

Work Appropriate

After graduating with an MBA from UW in Seattle, I started my career at one of the Big Four management consulting firms. I felt like I had finally made it. My longtime dream had come true; I was working in the United States of America! Here I was, entering the workforce after many adventures in my quest to secure a job. During the summer between the two years of my MBA program, I had the chance to go back to France and intern at one of the most prestigious strategy consulting firms there; however, I ended up turning down an offer to come on full-time. I'd wanted to remain and work in the United States. Thus began a series of whirlwind interviews that fall, as I met with most of the top consulting firms in the United States.

I don't remember all the interviews, but I do remember the one in Chicago, which was a branch of the same firm I had interned with over the summer in France. After learning I wanted to work in the

United States, the Paris office had given me a recommendation for the firm's office in Chicago. The morning of my final meeting in a series of interviews, I received a call from my mom in my Chicago hotel room.

"You must be done with your interview, right?" she asked.

"No, Mom, I am about to jump in the shower and head to the interview this morning. Why?"

"Oh, honey, I waited as long as I could stand to, but it looks like I messed up the time zone. Your dad passed away . . . two days ago."

"What?" I replied in shock. "*Two days ago? Is this a joke?*"

"No, honey, like I said, I waited as long as I could. I didn't want the news to impact your interview, and I guess I messed up."

"What happened?" I asked.

"It was sudden," Mom responded. "He was in the hospital for shoulder surgery. He started complaining about abdominal pain one morning, and by the end of the day, he was gone. The doctors think he had an intestinal obstruction, and, somehow, they didn't catch it."

I started sobbing but had to cut our conversation short when my half-sister started calling on the other line. I got the same story from her. She was devastated, and as much as I wanted to stay on the line to comfort her, I had to cut her off, too. I still had an interview to show up for and a job to secure. I believe that is what my dad would have wanted for me. I jumped into the shower, put on my interview outfit, and pulled myself together as I made my way to the office. As the recruiting manager welcomed me, I casually let her know that I had received bad news earlier that morning but assured her that there was nothing to worry about and I was still prepared to take the interview. I was holding back tears to the best of my ability, and she was horrified, telling me she would go get a partner to talk to me.

At that point, I thought I didn't need any special treatment and just wanted to do the interview as planned. The partner, a woman, came to meet me and asked me to chat with her in the bathroom. She told me that there was no way I was taking the interview that day. I pushed back, telling her that I had worked really hard for the interview, I had prepped, and I was ready. I could do it, I assured her, and the morning's events were not going to impact my performance. She refused and told me that the firm would help get me back on the plane and home to my family. I pressed further, insisting she let me do what I had come all this way to do, but she strictly refused. As much as it was understanding and supportive of her to help me get back home, I never got the job. A few months later, they invited me back for interviews, pretending they still had slots for the class of 2007, but as I sat in the waiting room alongside a bunch of undergrads waiting for internship interviews, I realized they had only asked me back out of courtesy. In hindsight, it was for the best. Eventually, I ended up accepting the offer for the firm in San Francisco instead, one that would allow me to learn much more and gain experience starting a new business. I have no regrets about that.

Once my new job was secured, I prepared for the big move from Seattle to San Francisco. A classmate of mine from the MBA program was also starting at the firm, and we planned to share an apartment together. To get ready for our new roles, we both decided that we needed a new work wardrobe. We drove about an hour and a half south of San Francisco to the outlets, where we splurged on different work outfits: pants, blouses, sweaters, shirts, skirts, dresses, and, of course, shoes. My de facto business casual outfit had always been slacks paired with a blouse or button-down shirt, so I stuck with what I knew. Quick piece of background on me: I have an hourglass figure. "Curvy" as some might call it, with large breasts and a booty. I've been this way since I was twelve, and I eventually learned how to dress for my body type. V-necks are the *best*.

After spending two weeks in Peachtree City, Georgia, for intensive training, my new roommate and I had our first week in the office, entirely devoted to HR training, office visits, and meeting our new colleagues. As part of the onboarding, we had to go over the dress code guidelines. I was scratching my head, trying to understand the need for this kind of training. Do people really need to be taught how to dress in work-appropriate clothing? Who would ever think it was appropriate to show up in leisure outfits such as shorts, tank tops, or flip-flops? The message of this seemingly needless training was clear: If in doubt, be conservative. Stick to dark colors and simple patterns, casual suits, shirts, and so on. Got it! I thought the new wardrobe I'd purchased at the outlets would fit in perfectly.

A few weeks later, after having gone through a few cycles of my newly acquired work outfits, I was called into a meeting in my HR manager's office. She gave no specific agenda for the meeting, so I proceeded to her office at the agreed-upon time and sat down across from her desk, wondering why I was there. The HR manager closed the door to her office behind her and started talking. At that point, I could sense that whatever she was trying to talk to me about was making her uncomfortable. Suddenly, it became clear: The issue was my cleavage. I found myself sitting in this meeting not due to any sartorial choice I had made but because of my *anatomy*! I sat stunned as she asked me to "think about" what kind of tops were appropriate for me to wear into the office and to be mindful of how much cleavage I displayed in front of my coworkers. The first thought I had was, *Where is this coming from?* I had been following the dress code guidelines as expressly told to me, and it apparently *still* wasn't enough. My second thought was, *I wear a 32E; how do you expect me to hide them?* Short of wearing a potato sack to work, I didn't know how I could possibly hide the boobs Mother Nature had given me.

Growing up, I had tried for a long time to hide my chest, and it never stopped anybody—including boys, of course—from noticing or making comments. As an adult now, I really thought I'd made it past juvenile commentary like this. I asked my HR manager earnestly what she expected me to wear or do in response to her feedback. Her only recommendation was to wear more "modest and flowy" tops. Screw this! That was *not* going to happen. After all these years, my boobs were becoming a problem again. I went home, thought the problem over, and found a way to turn a fake wardrobe issue into a real fashion statement. Just kidding! I had always loved scarves, and I realized that I could use them to cover my shoulders and upper body while still wearing the V-necks and other fitted tops I'd already spent money on. This is how my scarf obsession started, and as time went on, my collection kept getting bigger. Scarves became my main work accessory and one for which I am still known even years later. Rain or shine, you'd see me in a scarf at work. Coworkers and clients alike thought it was very "French" of me to wear scarves and it's true that I always found a way to make them fall in a very fashionable manner. If they only knew the real reasoning behind my fashion statement!

By this point, I have a collection of more than thirty scarves that I can use for any type of occasion—work, day, night, weddings, travel, and so on. I have so many that I try to stop myself from buying more whenever I see a new one that I like. A scarf addiction! Who'd have thought such a peculiar malady would come out of an equally peculiar piece of criticism about the "appropriateness" of my anatomy at work? As I reflect on that meeting, I think I would have handled it differently if it had happened today. I would have raised a stink and explained that I didn't choose this; I was born this way, and maybe instead of asking me to be more mindful about my choice of outfits, HR should have demanded that my coworkers stop focusing their attention on that part of my body! But in those days, it looked like my own natural assets had to be toned down in a US work environment. What a difference compared to the French manager I'd had during one of my internships, who'd literally made a comment about my breasts in front of all my coworkers. No toning them down back then . . .

Well, a little more than a year ago, I pulled the trigger and decided to have a breast reduction. It was time. I had talked about getting one since I was a teenager, but my mom, who is always right, opposed it and wanted me to wait until I'd had kids. By the time I turned forty, the "having kids" decision had been made back when I was twenty-seven or so, and my window to have kids was obviously slowly closing, so I decided to do a few consultations and see what it would take. After three different consultations with plastic surgeons, I was scheduled to have surgery in January 2023—fewer than four months after my last consultation.

Funnily enough, even though this surgery was something I'd always wanted, as the date drew closer, I started having a lot of anxiety about the surgery itself, about what I would look like afterward, and about losing part of the identity I've had since I was twelve. When the day arrived, my husband dropped me off, and there I was in preop, two hours before surgery. (I really wonder why they have you come so early, but I suspect it's just to have you fill out more forms reminding you of all the risks and potential complications. A great way to keep you calm and serene before surgery!) My anxiety was manageable, but I had to admit to the nurse that I was a bit on edge. "No problem," she said, "here are a few relaxers for you." Awesome, more drugs before being pumped with anesthesia. Time to take me to the OR. I remember wondering what the heck I was doing. Did I really need to go under the knife for this? Was it really necessary?

I don't even remember going under after they put the mask over my mouth and nose. Suddenly, I woke up and wondered if anything had happened. I had no cloudy head, no pain. I immediately looked down and realized my breasts were all bandaged. Crap, it did happen. I'll spare you the details of my recovery as there is nothing really to report. It went quite well. I was so excited to go shopping for bras and discover what size I finally was. I am happy to report that I am now a 32DD/34D. Yes, you read this correctly. Despite having asked to be closer to a C/D and taking almost a full kilo off my two breasts (that's more than two pounds), I am still a voluptuous D/DD. Am I disappointed, you wonder? Absolutely not. I think C/D would have been too small, and my new, after-market boobs are looking and feeling great. They just fit. But something else happened, too: I lost the need for that favorite accessory of mine that had defined my style for years. Yes, you heard it, I dropped the scarves, at least as a means to hide my breasts. I absolutely still have my full collection, but scarves are no longer my go-to disguise. My hourglass is now on full display, so take that, haters! I am no longer OEMed, but modified or not, I still rock quite the bodywork.

CHAPTER 8

I Guess in France Everyone Is Retired

A year into the job, I finally took my first vacation and joined my mom and her boyfriend at the time in Brazil. Excited about the prospect, I couldn't wait to get on the plane and explore what Brazil was all about. With that in mind, I left my work laptop behind but still took the only device I couldn't live without—my Blackberry. Remember, this was 2008, and the iPhone had barely come out; for security reasons, no company was issuing those yet. I spent two weeks between Rio de Janeiro and Salvador de Bahia with my mom showing us around the places where she used to live. Here I am, a few days into the trip, enjoying Copacabana, *feijoada*, and the sights of Rio, when I get an email followed by a call from work asking me—or more precisely, *telling* me—to fly to Reno first thing the Monday I was back.

Two things to keep in mind: Number one, I was literally taking a shower when the email and then call came in. I was half-naked and felt obliged to answer as I was still a rookie at that time and couldn't even imagine ignoring the call. How would it be perceived? I felt pressure to be available and to prove myself reliable. You can count on this worker! Number two, they wanted me to fly to Reno first thing the Monday morning I returned from vacation, even though I would be landing in San Francisco late the Sunday night before. So here I was, barely having started my vacation and already wondering how I was going to pull this off. No rest for the wicked American worker (again, I'm not complaining—I had it easy, and my experience can in no way be compared to the "real" American worker working on way more difficult jobs—think *Dirty Jobs* with Mike Rowe, every-one!). I ended up starting my journey on Saturday afternoon from Salvador and took a total of five flights to make it to Reno: Rio, São Paulo, New York, San Francisco, then Reno. No time for laundry and no time for jet lag. That was definitely the end of me trying to have a work-life balance. I didn't set boundaries, and that followed me throughout my time at the Big Four firm.

This experience got me started thinking about my new under-standing of work in the United States versus how things had been back in France. Generally, in France, people see the way Americans approach work as something like this:

- Americans live to work.

- Americans work extremely long hours, and sometimes they have two or three jobs.

- Americans have barely any vacation.

- Americans cannot afford to be out of work.

- Americans work too hard.

On the other hand, Americans perceive the way French people approach work like this:

- The French only work to live.

- The French barely work a full day.

- The French take a lot of breaks and two-hour lunches.

- The French take too many vacations. Don't count on them getting anything done in July or August!

- The French aren't worried about losing their jobs because they don't mind taking "handouts" from their government.

- The French don't like to work.

Of course, these perceptions are exaggerated generalizations designed to highlight the major differences in the way these two cultures perceive work. But if you ask your American and French friends about their perspectives on this topic, I am ready to bet that one or two of the aforementioned points will come up.

The truth is most of these opinions are bull crap! Let me tell you what I discovered through firsthand experience during my first ten years working in consulting at one of the Big Four firms in the United States.

- People in both countries work to live. However, more Americans are driven by the desire to feel successful in their careers.

- Americans do spend longer hours at work. The French tend to ensure they do not spend more than eight to ten hours at work per day. However, that doesn't mean that

Americans work *harder* than the French. During my experience working in consulting, I was often told by partners I worked with that I was the "most productive resource." I'd scratch my head, wondering how that could be since I do consider myself to be quite lazy. I know it sounds counterintuitive, but, despite my drive, I do not *like* to work. If I had the choice, I would prefer to travel, meet with friends, and have fun 100 percent of the time. I always find a way to get the work done efficiently so I can be done sooner rather than later. But, in my experience, a lot of Americans procrastinate at work. They get distracted very easily. They work on a task in fits and starts, surfing the web, making calls, or engaging in other tasks along the way, which leads to increased time spent at work. I am not claiming that all Americans procrastinate at work, but I do believe that they get easily distracted by things such as what's going on in the world, what their friends are doing, what they can buy today, or what they can invest in. I often caught my coworkers and colleagues on Facebook when they were supposed to be working on an assignment. It didn't make them poor performers; they just took longer to get the job done.

- On the other hand, the French do enjoy their breaks throughout the day and a long lunchtime. In my experience, while French and American workers might get similar amounts of work done during the course of a day, French workers spend the time they are not working on designated breaks for coffee and food, often socializing with colleagues. When they are at their desks, they are focused on work. Americans, however, spend the time they are not working sitting at their desks, busy on their phones or the internet.

- I do not want to spend too much time on vacation time and social coverage. With age, I have to admit that, working in the United States, I could certainly use more vacation time and more support in case I am unemployed or unable to work for whatever reason. However, I do believe there is flexibility in the United States to make it work.

I think I ended up with the best of both worlds: I learned how to be productive from the French method, which ensured that I would get things done in a shorter amount of time and keep my focus for hours on end. This skill came in handy when applied to the longer workdays in the United States, leading me to have increased productivity when compared to my peers. Perhaps that's one reason why I was able to get promoted so quickly at the Big Four firm. Who knows? In any case, this skill has rewarded my laziness (or lack thereof, depending on who you talk to). The less you work, the better off you are, right? You can take the girl out of France, but you can't take France out of the girl!

CHAPTER 9

Battle of the Coasts

When I was a kid growing up in France, I watched a lot of movies, especially American movies (dubbed in French, of course). I spent countless hours watching and rewatching those movies. Don't even ask how many times I watched *Grease* or *Dirty Dancing*! These audiovisual wonders shaped my perception of American culture before I experienced it firsthand, first at twelve years old. Then again at seventeen, for my high school graduation present, my mom agreed to send me to the United States for four weeks to stay with my brother's godparents in Lexington, Kentucky. I spent three weeks with them, hanging out at their antique shops, meeting kids my age, dating my first American boy, and then spending the last week with one of their friends as they were driving down to Florida. Their family friend was an elementary school principal, so I worked as a teaching assistant for five days in a K-1 class in Lexington. Interestingly, the teacher of the class was actually my brother's godparents' son!

Then finally, my most enduring experience of America was when I made the big move to attend UW at twenty-two. My understanding of everything, from American food to clothing, cars, the American way of life, and people's interactions with one another, was shaped by the silver screen. So, it shouldn't come as a surprise that I believed most Americans were loud go-getters, always in your face, brazenly speaking the truth without a filter. Does anyone remember Rachel McAdams' iconic line from *Mean Girls*: "God, Karen, you are *so* stupid!"?

I had always felt pretty confident I would fit in once in America. After all, I had often been told that I was pretty direct and that perhaps my filters were missing at times, both with respect to tone and body language. It's true that sixteen years ago, I had no care in the world about how people interpreted or felt about my words. What was the problem, so long as I was telling the truth? I had this idea that no matter how harsh the message, as long as I was being honest, people should be welcoming of whatever I had to say. If only it could be that simple.

The fact is that the impression I had gotten of American culture from movies turned out to be a myth. When I first landed in Seattle, I didn't want to hang out with other French people, hoping to improve my language skills by only associating with native English speakers, and so I openly avoided them. I didn't understand why someone who'd made the conscious decision to move to another country would immediately seek refuge in fellow citizens from their own culture instead of trying to integrate into the new one. After such a courageous decision, why would you chicken out and seek safety and reassurance? It seemed like a waste of time, one that wouldn't improve their English or their accents . . . and everyone knows how pronounced a

French accent can be in English. I may actually have miscalculated on that front, since I've been told my dating prospects might have been more prolific if I had kept my French accent. "I can always fake it," I used to tell my friends. "But I can't promise how long it will last. I really don't get the appeal." To persuade me, friends would compare it to meeting a cute American or Brit in Paris and ask whether it would be a turn-on to hear him speaking French in his native accent. "Of course!" I replied. "But the excitement would be more about riding off into the sunset to join him in America, or gaining access into the highest echelons of British society through him, no?"

My goal back then was to make friends of any nationality *except* French. And that I did, but I wound up mainly being friends with international students or other immigrants. I quickly experienced what they called the "Seattle freeze." I would meet countless Seattle locals, and they would always seem to be interested in learning more about me, where I came from, and the differences I had experienced since I moved to the United States. We would exchange numbers with the promise of an upcoming invitation to hang out more and I would eagerly await their calls. But they never came. And it would happen again and again—this pretense of wanting to hang out after an initial interaction but no follow-through ever came. What was that about? I actually started thinking the problem was me somehow, until one of my international friends shared the same experience. "It's not you. It's them. Haven't you heard about the 'Seattle freeze'? It's an established fact that it's especially hard to make new friends in Seattle." Scratching my head, I asked: "You're kidding, right? Why would they openly invite someone to hang out and then disappear? Isn't that rude? Why can't they just politely enjoy the conversation and move on?" Well, it turned out that course of action would be too direct for the introverts in the Pacific Northwest. I guess they prefer their coffee, trees, and politics.

But this was just one example I encountered along the West Coast. When I moved south three years later to San Francisco to begin my career, more West Coast traits emerged. One day, I was in the office meeting new colleagues and one of them straight up asked me if I was from the East Coast. "Are you from New York? Brooklyn?" I was flattered. I'd always wanted to live in New York, and I couldn't believe my accent hadn't betrayed me with my new colleague.

"Actually," I replied, "I am from even further east. Cross the pond and that's where I am from." He couldn't believe it and told me I spoke and behaved like a New Yorker. "What do you mean?" I asked.

"You are too direct to be from anywhere on this side of the country. Your looks and your accent make you seem like you're from Brooklyn or maybe Queens," he said. At that point, I was thinking, *Hell, fake it 'til you make it, lady. Maybe I can pull this off and make my way to New York after all.*

At the same time, I knew I needed to dig deeper into what my coworker had meant by my "not belonging to this side of the country." I asked him to tell me more about his impression of me in that respect. "There is something called being passive-aggressive on the West Coast," he explained. "People have a tendency to beat around the bush, not tell you exactly what they are thinking, wanting, or feeling. In most cases, if they're offended by something you've said or done, they'll retaliate behind your back by avoiding you and not following through on something they said they would do. They'll do this while smiling at you the entire time."

My most memorable experience of this phenomenon happened just a few years later. One day I was called to a partner's office where I found my HR manager sitting in the office, awaiting my arrival. That sight triggered an "I am getting fired and I don't even know why" response in my gut. It was well known at the firm that if you were called to a partner's office and HR was present, you were going to be let go. Here I was, arriving at his office, nervous, sweating, and thinking, *Well, this was fun, time to go find another job, I guess.* I sat down and an interesting dance began. The partner very delicately started mentioning that I was doing a great job, that the client really liked me and appreciated my work, and that I had also built up great relationships with the client team. By that point, it was starting to feel like a *really* weird way of getting fired. I kept waiting for the other shoe to drop, but it never did. Instead, I was asked to please take care not to become *too* friendly with the client. That if I ever accepted an invitation to go for a meal or drinks with the client's team members, I should make sure that another team member attended with me. I must have looked puzzled as I asked, "Did I do or say something in a client meeting that was perceived as informal, too friendly, or inappropriate in some way?" "No, no, no," the partner replied. "Just make sure that as you continue building a relationship with the client, you include your colleagues as well, so they all have a chance to grow their own relationships." Now I was confused. This didn't seem like the kind of meeting HR needed to be present for. I remember thinking that there might have been something else going on beneath the surface that I couldn't quite pin down. Fast-forward to a few years later, I discovered that someone had reported to HR that I had been sleeping with one of the clients! Apparently, whoever it was had seen me coming out of a hotel where a client was staying one morning and just *assumed* I had spent the night there. No one had ever come to talk with me about it first and instead had just gone directly to the top. After a thorough investigation, it had been determined that the accusation was baseless, my anonymous coworker had been reprimanded, and I'd had to endure this weird conversation, thinking the whole time that I was getting fired.

What stuck with me the longest was that I couldn't believe it took a full thirty-minute conversation and dancing around the subject at hand for a partner to indirectly tell me that I'd done something wrong, all without really telling me I'd done anything wrong. All the while, HR's presence indicated that *something* might have been seriously wrong, but it was still something that was never acknowledged directly in the room. Why all the cloak-and-dagger? Why not just tell me, "Be careful to be conscious of appearances. Certain actions can be misinterpreted. Today you are all good, but next time it could cause an issue for your employment. Be mindful of the impression you are giving others"? I guess that would have been too direct and might have been the cause of quite an uncomfortable conversation. But let's not go there!

Fast-forward a few years later, and I am still working at that Big Four firm, but with two partners on the East Coast, leading a sales pursuit for a major financial services client looking to transform their CRM processes and tools. Here I worked with the team, scoping, sizing, and pricing the potential project so it could be presented, first to the firm leadership for review and approval—it was a multi-million dollar proposal after all—and then to the customer for discussion in the hopes of closing the deal. I remember going through several iterations, especially on the resourcing and the pricing, and the two partners kept pushing back, wanting to keep the scope of work the same but significantly reduce the number of resources and, therefore, pricing. Anybody who knows me from that time knows I was not easily intimidated by partners and that I wouldn't keep my mouth shut if I felt we were not doing what was right for the people, the firm, or our clients. This was one of those times. They kept pushing me to bring the price down and I kept pushing them to take a hit on margin. Finally, on the last call, I ended up raising my voice and getting quite passionate about it.

So there I was, literally yelling on the phone, telling them this was not going to work, that it was not fair to ask the team to cut resources in order to get to a lower price point, and that they needed to suck it up and take a hit on margin if they really wanted to go in that low. And I will always remember their reaction: Neither of them was phased by what could be interpreted as my insubordination. They proceeded to tell me to calm down, acknowledging that I had made my case, and that I was right, and they would just take a small hit on the margin to come a bit lower. No tiptoeing around the bush, no hard feelings, no post-mortem feedback bullshit. Just two partners, as direct as they could be, knowing how to deal with the French in me and knowing that I was just trying to do the right thing for the firm. No HR intervention was necessary; no awkward meeting was scheduled. Just people sorting it out and allowing for my passionate French side, I guess. To be honest, after that call, I really thought I might end up in trouble. Again, who was I to raise my convictions to two partners over the phone like that? I still believe I wouldn't have been able to pull this off on the West Coast. Something would have happened after the fact—feedback, consequences, you name it. In a way, I picked the right partners to be myself and stand my ground with, for the firm and the team. And I am grateful because those two partners are still friends, even though we all moved on from the firm. And they have, on several occasions, been supportive of me joining their new firm. I guess honesty and directness can pay off. I learned to pick my audience, but I also learned the lesson that I might identify with New Yorkers after all. So maybe watching all those *Sex and the City* episodes actually paid off!

PART 3

Day-to-Day Life

CHAPTER 10

Healthcare in America—I Still Don't Get It

I remember landing in Seattle, back when I first moved to the United States, already aware before I even set foot on American soil that navigating the healthcare system would be one of the real cultural challenges I would face in this country. Fortunately, acquiring healthcare coverage through UW had been part of my admission process. Of course, it was also strange, because when I'd attended school back home, healthcare coverage had never been part of any school application. In France, healthcare is just a given because of the national health system. French citizens do, in fact, pay for their healthcare; it's just incorporated as part of their high taxes. For the three years I was at UW, I just used their provided healthcare plan. I couldn't afford private insurance anyway, but the university system was not bad. I think I got strep throat one year and another time I needed an ultrasound. Both times, getting care was quite easy: I just booked the appointment, went to the clinic or lab, and everything ended up being covered by the university plan I was on. I didn't end up paying for anything or the fees were minimal. It was a great plan for students, especially international students who have no clue about how complicated the US healthcare insurance system is.

But then, when I finally started a job, I needed to sign up for one of the plans offered by my employer. I had to figure it out. This was yet another "what the heck" moment. There were too many plans to choose from, and all those terms—"premium," "deductible," "co-pay," "POS," "PPO," "FSA," and so on—meant absolutely nothing to me back then. So I had to ask around my office, hoping someone would take the time to explain to me what all this meant. What did I need to select? What did I pay? What was covered and what wasn't? Choosing a healthcare plan was a daunting process, no question about it.

Ultimately, I was lucky, because at least my first job offered and subsidized healthcare. But I soon found out that my new insurance plan was nowhere near as good—or as low-maintenance—as my student plan at UW had been. I had to fight with my new insurance company to ensure they would reimburse what was due. One year, I had an abnormal Pap smear and the ob-gyn recommended that I get a colposcopy to make sure everything was fine. The lab results came back good, but my doctor asked me to repeat the procedure again and again for as long as my Pap smears came back abnormal—as a preventative measure against me developing cervical cancer. So I did. In fact, I did it every year for ten years straight! Well one of those years, without warning, the insurance company decided they were not going to pay for the procedure, even though they had done so for the last few years. I called them and I was told

I had a preexisting condition: HPV. Sorry, not accurate. I hadn't been *born* with HPV; I had acquired it like the majority of sexually active Americans. Yay for me!

So here I was on the phone, challenging my insurance company and explaining that the colposcopy was a preventative measure to ensure I didn't have cervical cancer. And preventative procedures were covered under my plan, right? Well apparently, not *this* one . . . The insurance company was essentially saying that since I'd had HPV in the past, it meant I'd *always* had HPV, and instead of paying for preventative screening, we'd just wait for me to have cervical cancer and then they would reimburse me in full for the treatment. Which, of course, would be thousands and thousands of dollars more than a freaking colposcopy! That makes *so* much sense. After multiple calls, I did what millions of Americans apparently do. They give up and just pay the bill. It was $600 for me. Thank God, I could afford it. But the experience also planted an idea in my head that I couldn't shake: What about people who couldn't afford to cover the cost?

Twenty years into this system and I'm still left with the same question. Twenty years later and I still don't get it. I still look at plans and think, *How much would I be spending out of pocket, and why? So, I can pay the deductible, but what about HSA and FSA, is that worth doing? Should I pay less per month and then put money aside or the reverse? Will this plan cover all my healthcare expenses? Oh, and none of these plans include vision or dental, so I'll have to go figure those out, too. Better not screw it up!* My experience of the US healthcare system is of a complicated web of decentralized payers, providers, and pharmaceutical companies, which, from my limited understanding, have pushed the cost of healthcare into astronomical figures. As if that wasn't enough, the COVID crisis exposed even more issues, including funding, preparedness, availability of patient information, and testing capacity—though I'm sure I'm forgetting some. In this time of great innovation, when is the United States going to seize the moment and make the structural changes required for all its citizens to receive the healthcare they deserve at an acceptable cost?

Don't get me wrong: I was born and raised on the other side of the Atlantic, and therefore I enjoyed the benefits of a universal coverage system. However, I have also experienced its limitations. While the French system is somewhat better in terms of cost, it is now running into other issues related to availability and quality. What Americans call "universal coverage" is a misconception. Yes, it is universal, but no, it is not free. And everyone can get care, but the system is not working that well these days. Let me explain: When I was growing up, we used to be reimbursed at a rate of 100 percent for any medical, dental, or vision service, procedure, or drug. Now there is a major deficit in the French government's budget, so only up to 70 percent is reimbursed, and you have to take additional private insurance to cover the difference. This budget deficit is the result of French citizens abusing the system. People with simple colds would end up seeing two or three doctors, while those with more serious illnesses went to five or six doctors for different opinions before pursuing treatment. They would just keep doctor-shopping, knowing full well that they would be reimbursed 100 percent of the cost, so they didn't care what that cost was. Even people who were not really sick went to the doctor. So now the country is struggling with a shortage of physicians, especially in rural areas, and hospitals do not receive enough funds from the government to function properly.

I am not pretending to have all the answers, but something between these two extreme models should be achievable. No solution would be perfect, but why couldn't we try to leverage all our innovative powers to totally break down and reconstruct what is clearly a broken system? Sure, it might be controversial and will certainly be opposed by lobbyists (another aspect of American life I still haven't fully grasped, as lobbies are not allowed in France). But how much more crisis, suffering, and financial hardship will need to befall Americans for something major to change? I am not making a political argument. This is not a plea for more government involvement or less of it. These are just the facts on the ground. For everyone living in America, the way forward clearly involves centralized or regulated coordination of community-based providers, ensuring that anyone in the country has access to affordable and consistent healthcare, regardless of whether they live in rural or urban areas.

Given my background, it should come as no surprise that I firmly believe technology has a major part to play in driving these changes. Most of us are aware of the importance and sensitivity of patient data, so why is it so difficult to get all your medical records in one place? If you want your test results or to see your medical history, you have to sign a release and sometimes pay a fee for your own medical records. Excuse me? I've already paid for the procedures, lab tests, and visits, and now you want me to pay extra to get what should rightfully be mine? It feels like your medical records are top secret documents doctors are reluctant to share for fear of . . . getting sued maybe?

Instead, why can't we follow the model other countries have established and create a secure patient health passport, which every individual would receive at birth and that would be updated with the patient's medical history—regardless of what provider they attended or where that provider was located within the country—until death? We used to have paper-based ones in France. (I still have mine!) These passports could allow *any* healthcare provider to access the patient data they need on an on-demand basis. No more filling out forms with all your medical history again and again for each new appointment with a provider, to say nothing of circumstances where you might require emergency care and may not be in a condition to provide that information. Each time you visit a healthcare provider, the purpose and findings of that visit would be recorded in your passport in perpetuity. Wait, isn't this something we should be able to do with blockchain-based technology?

Back in 2020, I was actually looking into leveraging blockchain to create a health passport. Then, someone I met told me that, in the United States, legally it is doctors who own patient data and not the patients themselves. If I wanted to move forward with this idea, I would need to look at pushing through a change in legislation first. I was dumbfounded. Was this real? This development was so discouraging that I didn't even bother looking into it any further. As I had during my experience trying to get repeat colposcopies covered by my insurance, I just let the idea go. Who was I to be able to bring about such change? Why does everything related to healthcare feel so insurmountable?

The unnecessary angst and confusion that seems to be built into the healthcare system in the United States became starkly apparent to me back in 2017, when I first brought home my furry kid, a dog named Taz. The simplicity of acquiring pet insurance for him was a revelation. Under most pet insurance programs, routine annual wellness exams and vaccines are not reimbursed, but everything else is covered at 80 percent of the cost after a $250 deductible. And our premium only runs us about $30 a month. It goes without saying, that the reimbursement process is fast and easy. Go to the vet, decide to pay upfront or not, submit your receipt online, and get reimbursed. All is done electronically, which reduces the cost of premiums even more.

So why can't we do that for humans? Why does it have to be so expensive and complicated for us? Let's keep it to a few deductible options, ensure everything is covered up to 80 percent, and off we go! There would be fewer administrative costs, fewer loopholes, and fewer incentives for hospital administrations to inflate the actual cost of medical procedures so they can make money off the insurance companies and the people. Everyone would still be making money. There is no reason *not* to simplify healthcare coverage this way. And there is no reason *not* to make it affordable to everyone—if you're willing to overhaul the entire system. It would not be free, but it shouldn't be anyway. I think there can be a balance between ensuring people's health is taken care of and turning a profit. Healthcare should not be seen as a social benefit paid for by the government but as a socially responsible business.

And please do not think I am advocating for the United States to move to the French model either. It is not viable. Those healthcare businesses should diversify their offerings in order to make more money outside of just insurance premiums, such as taking on pet insurance, providing wellness programs, and so on. They could think about people's entire life spans and design a business that would support them throughout their health journey. What a breakthrough, right? I am stating the obvious, and some insurance companies have been trying to do this, but it's unclear how successful they can be when there is no incentive to drive the cost down.

For me, hearing that Americans go bankrupt every day just for trying to stay healthy feels completely counterintuitive. In France, we are raised with access to healthcare no matter what and carrying insurance doesn't factor into whether a doctor will treat us or not. Living in the United States, whenever I quit a job or if I'm let go, the thought always crosses my mind: *What am I going to do?* I have been lucky to have a partner who can add me to his plan until the next job comes along. But for people who don't have that option, COBRA is outrageously expensive, and the marketplace can be problematic. For the unemployed, it is yet another hurdle to surmount when you're supposed to be focused on finding another job. You start thinking, *I'd better not get sick or break a leg, because my coverage lapsed.*

I think this is one of the reasons why the United States has a prosperous hustling culture. You have to in order to survive. You won't find that in France. Let me critique my fellow French citizens for a moment: People in France will stay on unemployment benefits for as long as they can instead of looking for a job. Why wouldn't they, when they can make almost as much on unemployment as they can working for a paycheck? The lack of a support system in the United States is a blessing and a curse at the same time. The hustle is real. Americans have to go find their next thing and even move for jobs if needed (well COVID might have changed that a bit!), which is something you rarely hear of in France. My mom always tells me, "Americans are so mobile. They'll go anywhere for a job." I have to remind her it's because they *have* to sometimes, not because they *want* to. No social safety net, no choice.

Both my heart and my head have a hard time with this. As I get older and more susceptible to illnesses, I wonder how I will be able to afford basic healthcare in my old age. Will healthcare ultimately become the trigger for me to spend my retirement in Europe?

CHAPTER 11

Gambling on Retirement

When I left France, I knew I was relinquishing my right to a French pension. That thought has been keeping me up at night since day one. Everyone who lives and works in France and pays their taxes is assured to get a pension. The amount you'll get is pretty much set, and you're more or less guaranteed to get it until you pass away, so there's no need—as there is here in the United States—to calculate the amount of money you'll need to retire or figure out what your life expectancy will be after you retire to determine how long you can afford to live on a fixed income. In France, the safety net is real. But for how long? This is my generation's question!

For the last twenty years, retirement has been a constant concern in the back of my mind. Whether starting a new job, exiting one, or taking a break from work altogether, I always live with the thought of what I must do to ensure I can retire comfortably. I am always dreading ending up in a situation where I cannot retire or cannot make ends meet in my retirement. Some of my career decisions over the years—especially when I was younger—have been driven by the fear of not being able to pay my bills or save for retirement. At the end of the day, the realization that you can work your ass off, save money, and invest it in the stock market and you can *still* completely fuck it up and end up with no retirement, having to work until you can't work anymore, is shockingly f-ed up. Over the years, this fear of mine has been revitalized whenever I have encountered the phenomenon of people in their seventies who've taken on "second careers" working at Walmart or other places to make ends meet long after they've retired from working in their original professional fields. Some do it for different reasons: to cover increasingly expensive healthcare, for additional "fun money," or just because they want to stay active. And then you contrast this with my mom back in France, who keeps telling me she'd love to live in the United States so she could keep working to get out of her boredom. First off, she wouldn't be able to survive half a day. I have to bring her back to earth: Many of her peers in the United States *have* to work in order to survive, but I doubt she completely grasps this. She's never had to face or plan for the lack of a safety net.

I don't know if it's fair to say that the French are in a constant state of retirement. The system was created in a way where French citizens accumulate years in order to retire with a full pension. Now they've moved to a point system. Every year, you pay taxes from your gross income, you accumulate a number of fiscal quarters during which you've contributed to the base pension fund and receive a number of points for the additional pension fund.

Funnily enough, I think I must have accumulated a point or two myself from a couple of paid jobs I did while a student in France.

I wonder how much I will be able to claim in the future—maybe twenty euros per month? I really have no clue. In order to collect your full base pension, you have to retire at sixty-four years old and have worked 172 quarters, which amounts to forty-three years. For the additional pension fund, you have to fulfill the base pension fund requirement before receiving those benefits.

In terms of the amount of money you will receive when you retire, you'll be comfortable. You are not going to get rich on retirement in France, to be clear. For the base pension, they look at the annual average of your best twenty-five years of gross income, the rate you are eligible for based on the total number of quarters you contributed, and the age you want to retire. So if you made 150,000 euros on average during your best twenty-five years, you worked forty-three years to fulfill your base pension, and you took your retirement after you're sixty-four years old (and I am simplifying), you'll receive roughly 75,000 euros per year in base pension. This amount is paid on a monthly basis, directly into your account. A lot has changed because of the government deficit and the demonstrations about the retirement age, but no matter what, if you have worked forty-three years in France, you will be taken care of.

Bear in mind, pensions aren't the only way that French people are provided for during retirement. There are many perks or discounts for seniors across France: Your tax rate is lower, and in certain cities, you get free public transportation or free admission to museums and other cultural institutions. And that is in addition to healthcare being covered! All the time, my mom informs me the French government is rolling out more and more preventative health programs for seniors, such as annual checkups, physical therapy, mental health checkups, and so on, to help prevent critical illnesses. Just talking about it with her makes me wonder whether I should try to retire, even part-time, in France.

But don't ever think about retiring in Paris. It is still extremely expensive, and a lot of Parisians end up retiring outside of Paris, away from the metropolis and its suburbs. They usually go back to the region where their family is from or just pick a place they really love. Usually, they choose somewhere the weather is a bit warmer and there is a slower pace of life. French people work to live, not live to work. Their mindset and their pace of living are different. There is more balance between work hours, vacation time, and holidays. The United States is a bit of a roller coaster by contrast.

When I arrived here, it was hard to grasp the concept of saving for retirement, especially using a 401k. The whole scheme was so foreign that I was left scratching my head again (the first time was with credit score, remember?) and wondering how anyone thought gambling with their savings seemed like a good way to prepare for retirement. From an outside perspective, it seems like the American government expects you to work hard, save money, invest it in the stock market, and pray that in thirty or forty years, your money will have grown enough so they don't have to support you beyond the bare minimum of social security benefits.

When I got my first job in consulting, I had the opportunity to open my first 401k account. But how was I supposed to know how to allocate my funds or how to pick mutual funds? No one taught me how to do that. And what *was* a mutual fund anyway? Having never done anything like this in France, here I was again in need of guidance. Yes, there is a stock market in France, and yes, we do know what stocks and SICAVs

(French name for mutual funds) are, but we do not have anything that really rivals Wall Street. And no one teaches us about investing in the stock market in France, either. It has always been regarded as a rich people thing. When I was growing up in France, no one would have told me, "Hey, start working, start saving, and invest in the market." Not even my dad would have, even though he was a more sophisticated investor with accounts at a Swiss bank. Even if he had any wisdom to impart to me in this arena, he never got an opportunity to do so. I had to learn after arriving in the United States that the stock market is a high-stakes gambling scheme. In order to make money, you have to take risks. The bigger the risk, the bigger the return. But guess what? It doesn't always work out, and you might lose everything. Hooray!

So, with only a few days left to make an allocation, this dumb French girl swallowed her pride and went to a coworker who'd started working around the same time but came from a finance background. I approached him, admitting I had a very stupid question, but I really needed help. I just acknowledged I had no clue about this 401k thing and asked him to help pick a strategy or define an allocation for me. He was gracious enough to explain how it worked and provided an asset mix that I should follow from an allocation perspective. And that is the story of how I made my first 401k allocation. He didn't tell me what funds to pick, so I still had to do some research, but at least I knew how much money to put into each category. He shared what I should be looking at, such as ratings, performance to date, performance year-over-year, fees, etc. He was talking about a bunch of concepts I had recently learned during my MBA, and I remember thinking I couldn't recall the meaning of any of this stuff . . . Good thing I hadn't picked a finance job!

The funny part is that I used that same asset mix he showed me for all my subsequent 401k setups until very recently. For more than ten years, I barely reallocated and kept my positions, hoping it would be enough. That is, until I was forced to start learning again, this time about target date funds, stocks, ETFs, and other asset classes. I also met my husband and started investing in real estate, which changed the game on how to secure retirement. But for a long time, I'd just been gambling with the few tips I had originally learned from generous colleagues or friends. Once I finally caved and got a financial advisor—and it took eight years—I realized this is a freaking scam if you don't know how to pick the right one.

All of this had been so confusing to muddle through. Now, I understand why there are programs that teach financial literacy in US schools. Your well-being is predicated on your ability to make money and ensure you know how to manage it properly to secure your retirement. So back to the American contradiction: Instead of paying high taxes and giving your hard-earned money to the government, which will eventually be given back to you in your old age—as is done in France—in America you get the opportunity to take that dollar and invest it in the market. I get the appeal. Governments are not the best investors or planners; so, sure, I would prefer to keep my dollars rather than allow the government to potentially spend them now on wasteful programs, hoping I will still get a pension in a few decades. Logically, it makes sense to ask people to invest in capital markets now when their invested dollars will most likely be worth way more in thirty years. The only problem with this is that capital markets are difficult to predict these days, and they don't always go right. You are heavily relying on people who have enough money to save and invest, get and stay minimally educated in financial markets, and hope their pot of money has turned to gold when it's time to retire. There are a lot of assumptions being made in that system, and most of them have been disproved by the United States. Look what happened during the recession in 2008 or with COVID in 2020. In both cases, people were about to retire, markets went bust, and they couldn't afford to any longer. They had to keep working or change their plans and hope the market would rebound. Unfortunately, crises are cyclical, so all of us must somehow plan for the next one, hoping it aligns fortuitously with our retirement timeline. Keep in mind you might have amassed enough money in your 401k to retire by a certain year, but your money is still locked in the market during your retirement, so you are still left exposed to market fluctuations. I get it, but I don't get it.

As a French woman immigrating to the United States, it all deeply concerned me—the way everything adds up, healthcare cost, no real retirement plan, not many unemployment benefits . . . You are really on your own. You are aware of the differences, but you haven't grown into the system, so you are at a disadvantage. You have to learn and plan quickly if you can. And at least for me, I still carry this fear, justified or not, not wanting to become a burden or having to go home to France. The fear of losing control of my financial future lingers. It is hard to come to terms with this model, especially when you come from Europe. At least for me personally. I believe it forces you to get into the hustle, despite already having made the decision to move to the United States and experience the hustle—I *did* sign up for it. You know what? The hustle is overrated. Maybe as I grow older and I hear about friends back home in France taking ten weeks of vacation, I think more about how I could use that time now.

When I do go on vacation, I check emails every morning, just in case. That's totally my fault—to be clear, no one is *asking* me to do so. But still, in the back of my mind, there is the unspoken expectation to do so. It doesn't matter what level you're at. You can be at the top of the ladder and still feel that way.

I have conflicted feelings. When I was twenty-two, I wanted to come to the United States to hustle and build a career. Now, at forty-two, nostalgia is kicking in, and I think it might be time to be closer to family and friends. Should I stay or should I go? But every time I think about it, I doubt that I would be able to go back now. I do not fit in with the French working culture anymore. I have become such an American with my salary expectations, work ethic, and the space I've become accustomed to. How could I go back to living in such small apartments? It is just a fact: I have assimilated so well into American culture that I doubt I would easily readjust to the overall culture in France, despite having grown up there. So, it will have to wait! Retiring back home sounds like a good plan—at least part time. When the time comes, finding a house in the south of France, Portugal, Spain, or Italy . . . why not? Maybe I can live my own version of *Under the Tuscan Sun*.

It's not lost on me that all of that would be made possible by my hustle in the United States. I doubt France would have allowed me to accumulate the same materialistic wealth or make any of the investments I've been able to, including starting my own business. For all its flaws, the United States does allow you to have such a diversified career, allowing you to work anywhere from large enterprises to small startups. The sheer diversity of things I've worked on, the travel experiences I've had, the people I've met, and the relationships

I've built—none of it would have been possible back in France, not in the same way. I think for me, at least, it would have been a hundred times harder back home. I am grateful for all the opportunities that the hustle brought me. I never minded when French people referred to me as "the American." I owe a lot to America. I made my way here, I stayed, I persevered, and I was rewarded for it. Despite some hard times, I can't quite yet come to terms with going back to France. I still wonder what I would be missing if I were to leave the United States, even during retirement. Maybe the best outcome for my retirement would be embracing and enjoying both sides of the Atlantic and having fun in the process.

CHAPTER 12

One God, Many Roofs

was born to a French, Moroccan-born Jewish mother and a Swedish, Polish-born Russian Orthodox father. I was baptized at a Russian Orthodox church in Stockholm, and a rabbi at a synagogue in Nice said a prayer for me after I was born. I consider myself a big French mélange, claiming a multitude of cultural backgrounds but no affiliation to any specific religion. My brother and I are, after all, the first generation of our family born and raised in France, and we happen to have been spoiled rotten because of this multitude of backgrounds. The combined religious calendars of France, Israel, and Eastern Europe provided us with plenty of benefits throughout the year. Since we went to a French public school, we had fifteen weeks of vacation, including eleven French holidays, seven of which are tied to Catholic holy days. At home, we would celebrate Easter twice and Christmas three times until I turned eighteen. We had Passover at Mom's and Easter at Dad's, but the best time of all was the end-of-year holidays.

They would start on December 6 with the German tradition of Saint Nicholas Day. Did I mention my dad was born in Gdańsk, Poland—then called Danzig—in 1927 to a Bulgarian father and a Russian mother? She herself had actually been born an aristocrat in what is now Ukraine back in the 1900s and was raised by a *kinderfräulein* (nanny). Apparently, we are part of the old Russian nobility. My paternal grandfather was even at Tsar Nicholas II's wedding!

Back to December 6. This day is traditionally a favorite holiday among German children because it is a gift-giving day. Every year, my holiday season started with a gift from my dad. It was always food-based, meaning we would receive cookies or candies, but what a treat it was to start that time of year with a gift! We then unfortunately had to wait until December 24 for the next gift-giving session. Depending on the year, we would split Christmas Eve and Christmas Day between my mom's and dad's homes, but that meant we got two trees, two dinners, and twice as many gifts. I am sure I would have preferred for my parents to still be together at that point, but you must take what you can get. And why not take advantage of not one but *two* Christmases?

After Christmas, we would get to celebrate New Year's Eve. And until we were teenagers and began rebelling against our parents, we had to celebrate it *twice*. New Year's Eve with one parent and New Year's Day with the other. My dad would usually just take us out for a meal and a movie or to a museum exhibition in Paris. And with that, you would be forgiven for thinking the holiday season was over. But you would be mistaken.

Both the French Epiphany and Russian Orthodox Christmas fall on January 6 of the new year. In France, this is when you gather for the king cake (*la galette des rois*—not the New Orleans kind), another celebration loved by children. Inside the cake, a figurine is hidden and whoever gets the *fève* wins a prize and the king's crown. For my non-French dad, January 6 was "real" Christmas according to the Gregorian calendar. The tradition was to have a house party and cook a very large lunch or dinner for his Eastern European friends. My brother and I would always be part of those celebrations, having the privilege of helping my dad prepare for it—which wasn't actually that much fun as a kid—but also eating a large amount of food and receiving, yet again, a small gift as an acknowledgment of this special day. We would usually be two of the handful of kids present, and if the guests were generous that year, we would get even more gifts from them as well. That is what it was all about. And then, the holiday season was finally over. But not the gift-giving one!

My birthday, and my dad's, would come fourteen days later, on January 20. Yes, I was born on Inauguration Day. That year no one was sworn in, but since I've moved to the United States, it is my absolute pleasure, every four years, to welcome a new US president on my birthday. It started with George W. Bush; however, neither he nor any of the subsequent presidents have ever made an appearance at my birthday celebration. Nor have any of them invited me to their Inauguration Ball—but what a gift it would be!

Sharing a birthday with my dad was always weird for me as a kid. On the day I was supposed to be the center of attention, I had to show respect to my elders by picking up the phone and calling my dad. Do you ever think he would do that first? No way! My dad was old school and from a different era. He would always wait for me to call to wish him a happy birthday before he even wished me the same. All this drama every year—when January 20th wasn't even his real birthday! After he passed, we found a copy of his birth certificate listing *June* 20, 1926. The story goes that, during World War II, he had to falsify his date of birth in order to get into the Russian army and for his military allowance to be sent back to the family. I am not sure how much of that story is true. My dad was twelve or thirteen when the war started. The Soviet Union lowered its conscription age from seventeen to sixteen after entering the war in 1941. Did he make himself younger to avoid conscription until 1943? Unfortunately, I do not have the answer. He passed before I could ask. Despite this peculiar situation each year growing up, my (our?) birthday would mark the end of the almost eight-week period of constant celebration and gift-giving that the holiday season brought us kids.

When I arrived in the United States in the fall of 2004, a lovely family from Seattle (friends of friends) agreed to host me for a week until I could find a place to live. They picked me up from the airport on a Tuesday evening, a couple of days before my student orientation at UW was about to start. I was exhausted from the trip, and that first night, their house felt like a refuge. It was different from what I had experienced after spending time in Kentucky, but also surprisingly similar. The house was an eclectic but comfy cottage in Ballard, which smelled of unfamiliar but pleasant cinnamon. I got to sleep in the furnished basement on a built-in bed that felt like a retreat from the outside world, and I felt grateful to be warmly welcomed. After a few days, I learned more about the family I was staying with. He was, and still is, a successful tax accountant; she was, and still is, a pastor. I remember wondering what it meant and if she would turn out to be like the ones featured in American movies—more preacher than a religious guide—and whether I would have specific rules to follow during my stay with them. I was thinking of a Joel Osteen type of preacher, a preacher whose televised sermon millions of people tuned into every Sunday, a wild-looking preacher shouting and gesticulating across the stage to invigorate the crowd of followers, closing with one more request for donation or a purchase at the end. That idea is what I would call the "American Dream" version of God: Preach the Word of the Lord, don't abide by His Word, but make millions in the process.

This preacher who hosted me was the total opposite. She was calm, poised, warm, generous, sensible, and understanding. I only had one rule to follow: I had to join them at church on Sunday. That first Sunday of my new American life, I proceeded to join them for my first Presbyterian church service. This is the day everything got a bit fuzzy. What is a Presbyterian church? Remembering from my school studies, I knew that they were part of the Protestant branch of Christianity, but what, in God's name—no pun intended—did it mean? It was explained to me that there were many Protestant factions. At one point, they had all belonged to the Catholic church, but they disagreed on the rules of their faith and their approach to God and so decided to go their separate ways. Presbyterians were one of those denominations, but let's not forget the others: Baptists, Episcopalians, Evangelicals, Lutherans, Methodists, Pentecostals, Anglicans, Quakers, and the list goes on. Add to the Protestants, the Catholics, Greek and Russian Orthodox Christians, Jews, and Muslims—and the list is enormous but still incomplete. Like everything in America, there is a different flavor for everyone, and you are sure to find something that suits you. What is even a little scarier is the fact that organizations such as Mormons and Jehovah's Witnesses are not considered cults or sects like they are in France and that the Church of Scientology has places of worship—more like stores—on the main streets in the United States, visible to all. I was raised in a secular country where religion was quite simple: You belonged to one of the three main religions—Christianity, Judaism, or Islam—with a few possible offshoots. An absolute legal ban is in place on any belief systems requiring you to pay into it, which are termed "cults" or "sects." Why the need for so many organized religious groups?

What added to my puzzlement was the fact that religion played a larger role in the fabric of American society. It's everywhere. Every state has a constitution that mentions God, the divine, or a "supreme being." The Pledge of Allegiance includes the line "one nation under God." Even the money Americans use to pay for things has "IN GOD WE TRUST" printed on it. Churches all over the country are a hub of community, spawning book clubs, community events, and lifelong support. Religious beliefs regulate American bodies. Pastors preach what to do with your sexuality and how to cast your vote from the pulpit. Of course, depending on which faction you are affiliated with, the scope of control and influence varies. But it all still boils down to a group of people who use His Word to regulate other people's lives. Do they look at themselves in the mirror?

As I contemplated applying for US citizenship, I figured I'd better get with the program and get comfortable with trusting one God and entrusting my body and mind to one of these factions and their ever-present influence in politics. Funny story, at least I can't become Mormon without going willingly. The Mormons have a deal with the Jewish community where they're not allowed to convert

Jewish people to the Church of Jesus Christ of Latter-Day Saints after their death (yes, this was a real thing that was happening).[1] I guess I am safe from them at least. But which religious faction would try to bring a French-Jewish-Russian Orthodox girl into the fold anyway? Sinner that I am, am I a lost cause for these groups? Perhaps not. I am baptized: check. I don't really believe in God, at least, not as it has been packaged by the three mainstream religions, and I do not go to church. I think the world is round and my scientific, rational mind does believe and understand that natural selection is real. We do descend from apes, and we are no more special than other animals that have lived on this planet. For your information, I have two dogs, and I do believe both the rainbow bridge and doggy heaven exist!

Here I was at my first Presbyterian church service, looking out toward Lake Union, being welcomed as a French-Jewish-Russian Orthodox girl currently staying with the pastor's family while starting as an international student at UW. Welcome applause! The service started and I was standing up on cue, singing along as required, and trying to make sense of the day's sermon. It was quite pleasant, the message was straightforward, and the after-service coffee and food were a nice perk. I started thinking that most people must be coming to church for the after-service experience—catching up with others in the congregation over a hot beverage and amazing sweets. The kids ran around, the adults chatted, and after an hour or so, churchgoers began to go their separate ways for Sunday lunch. It's all about the experience, which was a big difference from churchgoing in France. Back home, you show up to church on Sunday morning, you go through

---

[1] Associated Press in Salt Lake City, "Holocaust victims and Queen Mother posthumously baptized by Mormons," *The Guardian*, December 21, 2017. https://www.theguardian.com/world/2017/dec/21/mormons-holocaust-victims-baptism-lds-church

the hour-long Catholic mass, mainly in Latin—we need to keep those traditions—and you get the hell out of Dodge after dropping a few euros to help support your congregation. There was no hot beverage, no food, and no kids playing around after mass. No wonder religion has been declining in France!

To my surprise, my native and adopted countries seem to be on opposite sides of a spectrum: On one hand, you have the openness of the United States with its abundant number of religious denominations and organizations, most of which are telling people what to believe and how to live their lives, because "God knows best." Every public space is up for grabs as a stage to push their ideas and beliefs, no matter the veracity or consequences. On the other hand, France, in all its chauvinism, actually practices what it is preaching: Believe and follow what suits you, but for Heaven's sake, do not feel insulted if we disparage it, and do not bring your beliefs into the public domain. In France, they don't care what floats your boat as long as you don't try to rock anyone else's. Religion is a private matter, and it should stay that way.

Now, you might say I am oversimplifying, and you're absolutely right! I was taught that there is only one God, but I can't stop wondering whether all the Gods of this world agree with the roofs being put over Their heads!

After moving out of my host family's house, I continued going to church almost every Sunday for that first year so I could still see them and stay in touch. I was always welcomed, and I always politely followed the cues to stand and sing as the service required. Despite experiencing such a lovely time every Sunday and using that time to reflect, it never really changed my thoughts on religion. I didn't find

God, but I do like going window-shopping at America's religious grocery store. If I ever do find my faith, I can rest assured that there is a flavor for me out there!

CHAPTER 13

Volunteering? What's That?

nterestingly, I didn't think about nonprofits or volunteering until I started working with my editor on this book. But that was yet another area in which my mind was blown when I first arrived in the United States. With the largest nonprofit "sector" in the world, North America easily doubles the European efforts. The amount of corporate donations is so high that it is almost unbelievable. During my first year in engineering school, I was oblivious to this phenomenon, but once I started the MBA program, I received a small scholarship from the MBA fund and began attending networking events organized by large corporations. At that point, I almost fell off my chair when I realized the time and money those organizations pour into those initiatives. Years later, I learned this monumental effort comes with its advantages—meaning tax breaks. And who doesn't like tax breaks? But I still had to believe that some of the largest foundations must also have been created to use the enormous wealth they generate to do some good.

Once you dig into the matter, you will swiftly learn that the American government doesn't subsidize as much as in France. I think that is a major difference. Don't get me wrong, France also has plenty of nonprofits as well, but not to the extent of the ones found in the United States. People in France might give once a year to the telethon, a twenty-four-hour fundraising TV program, during which thousands of participants, including celebrities, entice people to call and donate toward research for rare genetic and progressive diseases. When it first started, people had to call the phone lines, but now the process is digital, though they still run twenty-four hours of entertainment, documentaries, and shorts. That's really all there was when it came to nonprofit fundraising when I was growing up. But then, in the mid-80s, the famous French comedian Coluche created "*Les Restos du Coeur*," a food bank for people experiencing homelessness. Since then, more French celebrities have started their own foundations or nonprofits to help causes that matter to them. Not being a part of French high society, I never ran into fundraisers or heard about people making very large donations to the arts or anything like that. Even large companies would not publicize or encourage their employees to donate money or spend time volunteering—that sort of thing would be done outside of work, a personal investment of time and money. Even when I went back to Paris in the summer of 2006 for my MBA internship, the firm I worked for didn't mention anything about community engagement. This was not the kind of thing companies were openly talking about or supporting in France.

After moving to the United States and discovering all the money flowing from companies and people to nonprofits, I started wondering why this country still had any problems. I do believe Americans are more generous with their time and money. There is a greater sense of community here compared to Europe. It is a contradiction—the individualistic nature of the United States when held next to this drive to come together to support a cause, the arts, or a community in need. It almost seems as if the lack of a social safety net has unintentionally instilled in Americans a desire to provide support and help to one another. At least, that is the perception I've gotten over the last twenty years. It is almost ingrained in the people here. By contrast, volunteering is quite rare in France. We are not taught to do this at all. Perhaps it is yet another aspect of the American hustle—since you can't count on the government to help you in your time of need, your community will band together to ensure there is a structure to support the less fortunate or the arts or the animals.

Again, we have a few organizations, such as the Red Cross, the Salvation Army, and EMMAUS, which is much like Goodwill, created by yet another priest, Abbé Pierre. But nothing reaches the scale of such organizations in the United States. It's quite amazing.

Because of France's high taxes, I think it's considered a given that the government will subsidize nonprofits with taxpayer money. Therefore, perhaps French people do not feel like contributing above and beyond. And even if they do, it is nothing compared to the United States and the billions flowing into the nonprofit industry. In the United States, the average donation in 2020 was around $2,500 per family and $471 billion overall.[1] Compare that to France, where the average donation in 2020 was around 560 euros per family and 8.5 billion euros overall.[2]

---

[1] Taylor Schulte, "Charitable Giving Statistics for 2023," *Define Financial*, February 10, 2023, https://www.definefinancial.com/blog/charitable-giving-statistics/.
[2] Daniel Bruneau, Anne Cornilleau, and Adèle Pellet, "National Giving Landscape," Fondation de France, September 2021, https://www.fondationdefrance.org/images/pdf/synthese_gen21ANweb.pdf.

One of my first experiences volunteering was during that second trip I took to the United States to spend four weeks with my brother's godparents in Lexington, Kentucky in the summer of 1999. The last week they'd planned to drive to Florida for an antique show. Yes, they were big into antiques, finding pieces, restoring them, and reselling them. So, once they'd left town, I had to spend my last week with their close friend, whom I'd met during my first trip in 1994, and she generously welcomed me with open arms. As the principal at an elementary school that was starting that week, she asked me whether I wanted to come and assist in a K-1 grade classroom and just help with the kids. I immediately said yes. I was seventeen and a half, and I had never taught kids before but I thought it would be a good experience. They paired me up with another assistant, and together with the teacher, the three of us were all set to manage the first week of school.

That week was my first real encounter with the school bus experience. I didn't have to ride the school bus myself, but I also hadn't realized that there were specific school bus routes that picked up kids and dropped them off at school, all at once, around 7:30 a.m. and then picked them back up again around 2:00 or 2:30 p.m. to drive them back home. In France, we do not have this kind of bussing system, as most students take public transportation to and from school. Getting to school early to welcome the kids as they arrived on the bus was a totally new experience for me.

I also learned that this particular school was in a really rough part of Lexington and largely served kids from economically challenged communities, mainly African Americans. I learned that some students' families suffered from food insecurity. As a result, the school had raised funds to provide breakfast and lunch for those kids who couldn't afford it. This was the first time I had run into this kind of community program, and seeing firsthand the reality of wealth disparity in the United States was also new. The principal had to explain to me the situation the school was in, what they were trying to do for their students, and the harsh reality of people living in one of the richest countries in the world who still could not afford to feed their children. These are the aspects of American life that the movies I remember from that time were not portraying. I was clueless, thinking such things would never happen in France—kids coming to school on empty stomachs, schools paying for breakfast. All teenage me knew was that meal plans were subsidized by the school, and parents had to pay for lunch—that was all. No one in France would go out of their way to ensure the kids at school had a full stomach in the morning. Maybe on a case-by-case basis, but not on the scale of an entire school.

It was such an eye-opening experience on so many levels. But the two main takeaways were the reality of America still having communities that cannot make ends meet and the sense of community—in this case, a school—coming together to help. Nothing I had experienced in France compared to how amazed I had felt at that Lexington school's commitment to supporting those kids.

My reward in all this was that a few kids became really fond of me in those five days. It was so cute. I remember getting their attention and them wanting to sit next to me because I was French. I was their entertainment for five days, really. They would ask me where France was on a map, and when I showed them, they couldn't believe I'd flown over an ocean to get there. A lot of them had never heard about Europe, and why would they? When your family struggles to provide basic needs like food, no one should expect you to be able to put France on a map. They would also ask questions about whether we ate pizza in France, too, whether we played baseball, or what was on TV. It ended up being hard to leave after only five days. I just hope that I made a good impression on the kids and that it opened up their world a bit. And who knows? Maybe some of them were bitten by the travel bug just from hearing about where I came from. One can hope!

Most people back in France do not know this side of America. They see Americans as successful, greedy money-hoarders who want to tell Europeans what we should do politically. We have no awareness or visibility into the reality that many Americans do want to make money, and sometimes a lot of it, but they also want to give some of it back. Yes, for tax-break purposes, but does it really matter? But not only that. When you think about the amount, it is a means to an end. Regardless of how a donation to a nonprofit affected the donor's taxes, the reality is that some research or breakthroughs or movements or programs would not have existed without that money, period.

And once you benefit from the system, you feel like you have to contribute, too. Every year since I started working in the United States, I have contributed to the MBA scholarship fund to honor the help they gave me, even without me really asking. And it was helpful, for sure. It is the kind of generosity that compels you to do the same. Once I started giving back, I also began looking for other causes I might want to help monetarily, too, such as organizations that support the arts, culture, animals, or kids. And again, I realized all of it is primarily privately sponsored. All of those plaques on the walls of museums, on benches in parks, or on other cultural landmarks and resources represent major corporate donations and a lot of individual donors. In my case, I hope one day I can contribute at a level that gets my name on a wall, not so much for the fame but for the knowledge that I helped keep an institution open to carry on its mission.

CHAPTER 14

At Your Service ... Not Likely

My first visit to the United States in 1994 was also my first time experiencing US customer service. I was twelve years old, and my mother, brother, our host, and I were shopping at a *fancy* Ross store. I thought the discount department store was the coolest thing ever, as we didn't have discount stores like that back in France. I remember buying my first pair of Calvin Klein jeans there, along with a couple of tops, including my first tank top! I felt like I was on top of the world. I was taking my first steps into the world of fast fashion by picking out a casual outfit at Ross. Don't laugh . . . I was so naïve and excited that this was a really big deal for me.

As I was browsing through clothes, a woman approached me with a huge smile and started asking how I was doing and if there was anything she could help me find. Immediately, I started thinking, *What the heck does she want from me?* I politely replied, "No, thank you, I'm just browsing." *Are you actually trying to help me?* I wondered. That would certainly never happen back in France. Even in the actually fancy Galeries Lafayette, a famous Parisian department store, no one ever came to check on you to see if you needed help shopping. You'd have to almost beg to get any assistance, and even then, it might not be pleasant. There, employees act as if you are an inconvenience as a customer. You're meant to just pick something off the rack and hope for the best, and good luck if you cannot find the item you are looking for, need another size, or want another color. Making a sale does not feel like the store's priority in France.

But in America, apparently, it was the opposite. The whole shopping experience was such a culture shock that, for the rest of my trip, I ended up trying to avoid sales associates wherever we went. We would go into a store, and I would purposely avoid making eye contact with them, hoping they would not talk to me. Honestly, to this day I'm *still* not comfortable with the experience. I don't try to avoid sales associates anymore so much as I've learned to keep them at bay. If someone comes my way, asking me how I am doing and if there is anything they could do to help, I have my canned answer ready: "I am good, thanks. What about you?" It seems to surprise them that someone is actually asking them how *they* are doing for once, and they usually thank me for asking. That's when I drop the, "I am just browsing, thank you" line, and I'm basically guaranteed to be left alone for the rest of my shopping trip.

The other mild shopping anxiety that I still experience, despite having lived here for almost twenty years, kicks in whenever I need to ask a sales associate for help. Even if they volunteer to help at the beginning of our interaction, once I do actually need something from them—like a different size, for example—I still have this feeling that I'm going to bother them by asking. I'm still uncomfortable, thinking it's going to take a huge effort for them to provide me with what I need in order for me to potentially buy. Then I see Americans come into stores and just go for it. They storm in and ask for what they want: "Do you have this item in-store? In my size? In a different color? Oh, it's online only. Can I order it with you and get it shipped here?" I think to myself, *My god, these people are so demanding.*

Great cultural conditioning from France, right? I'd like to think I am the easiest customer out there since I haven't been raised with the same expectations of options and help as Americans have.

I must also admit that I have bought stuff in the past just because I felt bad for the salesperson who helped me. I didn't want them to have wasted their time on me and missed out on commission. I know it's silly, but I've definitely fallen into that trap. Last year I was back in San Francisco for a wedding. Once my husband and I arrived, I realized I hadn't packed the right kind of bra for my outfit, so after securing the right bra at Target, I ended up at Barneys and thought I would browse around just for fun. We had another wedding to attend in England a month later, so why not? This lovely woman came my way and asked if I was looking for something special. I literally answered, "Not really, I have a wedding to go to, but I am all set." She jumped at this opening, suggesting I try something on—just for fun, of course. Next thing you know, I was in a fitting room trying on three different outfits, and she was running around bringing me different sizes, yet another kind of bra, and matching heels. Half an hour later, I left the store with a new outfit for the wedding! I felt so bad about taking up a dressing room and spending so much of her time that I felt like I *had* to buy something. I justified it by thinking, *You know what? I'm just going to treat myself!* When I got back to the hotel, my husband rolled his eyes, shrugged his shoulders, and scratched his head at my peculiar shopping choices. And it's true, I really didn't need to buy these things, but I kept justifying my purchases, thinking I'd wear the new outfit to the other wedding and whatever other events I might attend over spring or summer. Well, guess what? It's been more than a year, and I haven't worn it again. Pathetic! I guess I am embracing my American side—buying things I do not need!

It looks like I brought my American side back to France last year, too. While it may be true that no one at a regular store in France will come and ask if you need any help, at a luxury store, it is a different story. One of my dreams in life was to buy myself a pair of Louboutins. I had gone to the store several times in Paris and always left empty-handed. Who needs such an expensive pair of shoes? So, during my visit last year, I thought I would make my usual pilgrimage to Christian Louboutin and check out their latest pieces of art for fun. In the store, they asked me to wait for a sales associate to become available to assist me, and once she arrived, she immediately asked me what I was looking for. I had been eyeing a specific pair of heels that summer and thought I would ask if they had my size so I could at least try them on—for fun. I was disappointed when they didn't have them, but I realized this was my way out. "No problem," I told the saleswoman. "I actually live in the United States and will look for them there." I thought, *Thank God I will not be spending that amount of money on a pair of shoes! I am safe.* But not so fast! The sales associate started explaining that she had plenty of American customers and whenever they visited Paris, they came in and bought a pair of shoes here to avoid sales and import taxes in the United States. Now I was intrigued, so she calculated for me how much the shoes would be in the United States and then compared that figure to how much they would cost me if I bought them here in France, thereby avoiding the 40 percent luxury import tax. She then informed me that I could get the sales tax refunded back at the airport. I was sold! This is how I bought my first pair of Louboutins, which I then had to haul all the way back, box and all, to where I lived in Austin. My American side just couldn't say no to a good deal and a very nice sales associate ... shameful, really!

The other major differences in terms of service between France and the United States are in the restaurant business and are two-fold: quality and length of service. When I first arrived in the United States, I was surprised by the level of friendliness we received when getting a table at a restaurant, being seated, and then being taken care of. The server would be welcoming, sharing their name and mentioning they would be taking care of us that night. Then, they would ask whether we wanted water—sometimes a choice between flat or sparkling—and whether we were ready to order our drinks. They would then politely give us time with the menu and come back to take our orders. If you needed a recommendation, they were open to providing one. This is not anything like what you get at a typical French restaurant. If you go to a café, you must catch a server's attention to even be seated. Then you sit, and it takes yet another ten to fifteen minutes for someone to come and ask you what you want. It's actually quite outrageous, this lack of attention when you think about it. I am guessing it must be a bit upsetting to foreign tourists, too. It pisses me off whenever I go back, and I have to flag down a waiter for them to come and ask me what I want to drink or eat—as if being a paying customer doesn't matter at all!

Again, the young me didn't realize that waiters and waitresses were paid such a small hourly wage in the United States and relied on customer tips for most of their take-home pay. In France, it is the reverse. Waitstaffs are paid decently, so barely anyone leaves a substantial tip. I definitely think this drives the different behaviors. If you need to make at least a 20 percent tip, you need to provide great service. If you don't rely on tips, you can afford to put much less effort into serving customers. Most of the great service you get in France is at higher-end establishments, while your day-to-day watering holes will not provide remarkable customer service experiences. In fact, you'll be fighting for your life to get any type of friendly service. It's almost like survival of the fittest: The most resilient will get what they need. I am exaggerating a bit, but you catch my drift.

As I've lived in the United States and returned to France once a year on average, it has been interesting to experience this kind of service now as an outsider. Being French with an American accent in English and having acclimated to an American level of service, I find the servers back in France do not like me. First of all, whenever I go back, I'm usually with my husband or an English-speaking person, so waitstaff think I am American at first. Then when I switch to fluent French with obviously no accent, they are horrified and usually pissed as if they've been caught. They thought they were dealing with tourists, but no, I got ya! I'm the member of the dining party, then, dealing with menus, ordering, asking about water and bread for the table, you name it. I think the French servers feel like they've been tricked, given they can get quite mad, but I don't think it's smart to make assumptions about people. And if they were focused on the quality of their service, it wouldn't matter anyway. But that's not what they do, and it seems like they end up being nicer to tourists than French people, unfortunately. Tourists are important for business—French people, not so much! Tourists might tip, but French people won't. All in all, I have to admit that, in that sense, I prefer the US model. It makes for a better experience and a better time dining out.

The system here in the United States is, of course, not without its flaws. The focus on service is high, but one custom that always bothers me is when the servers take the empty plates away from some diners while others in their party are still eating. This is the most awkward thing to me. I really don't get it. In France, the wait-staff tries to bring the plates for everyone at the same time and they will wait for everyone to have finished their meals before taking the plates away. You are all dining together, so they try to make your shared experience as similar as possible. Here in the United States, one person may end up having no plate in front of them while their dining companion is still eating, resulting in an awkward situation where one person watches the other eat while they look like they're ready to get the check and leave. I'm not certain of the etiquette behind this US practice, but it always makes me scratch my head. I find it disruptive, especially when they interrupt a conversation to ask whether you are finished eating or not. I feel like they're rushing me out the door. This would never happen in France. If servers started to pull empty plates while the whole party wasn't done yet, someone would immediately say something or complain. Anyone who finishes eating before their friends would simply continue the conversation and just wait for the others to finish their dish before all empty plates were cleared away. No big deal. The same principle applies at home if friends come over for dinner. It feels like this practice all comes down to the restaurant trying to turn tables over as soon as possible, trying to get diners in and out as fast as possible to increase the number of tables served per night.

The amount of time allotted for diners to finish their meals in the United States is also something completely ludicrous to me. When making reservations at a restaurant, I've often seen the disclaimer, "Be aware the reservation is for one and a half hours." What is this? What is it to the restaurant if we spend more time and more money? Does it matter? What issue are we causing? Apparently, the issue of primary importance to a restaurant in the United States is not the experience diners have enjoying themselves and hanging out with their friends; it's how fast they can turn over tables to make the maximum amount of money and tips per night!

Even twenty years later, this issue still bothers me every single time. I still do not get it. I feel rushed through dinner and when I check my watch, I realize I've barely spent forty-five minutes from start to finish for a full meal. What? For the price I am paying, this experience isn't worth it! Despite the great, attentive service, dining out in the United States is overall not an enjoyable experience for me. The rush to get people in and out of the door ruins it. In France, restaurants actually allow people to stay for at least three hours, and waitstaff have a hard time asking people to leave. Eating out turns into a whole outing. Don't get me wrong: I have caused problems in my youth by staying way past the allotted time, continuing to order beverages, desserts, and coffees—but it was delightful. Not having to think through what the next course is, talking at length with friends, forgetting what you want to order, and just enjoying a good time.

The latest of those occurrences actually happened in the summer of '22, when I spent a few days in Paris after not having been back for a while. I finally had the opportunity to meet up with a friend I'd only met before on Zoom during COVID. We organized lunch one day, agreeing to meet around 12:30 p.m. I had the clarity of mind not to plan anything between our lunch and a late dinner I had scheduled with another friend. It was a good call on my part, as despite my fifteen-minute late arrival for lunch (I'd been waylaid by my visit to Christian Louboutin, which she found hilarious), we ended up staying at the café's terrace for seven hours just eating, drinking, and catching up about everything and nothing. The café was in a prime location in the center of town, yet they didn't kick us out. I can only assume we didn't end up consuming as much as they would have hoped, but it was raining, and diners were coming in and out, and the servers just didn't care. I am sure they lost money on our table since we ended up drinking water as we waited for the rain to stop. I hadn't done that for a very long time, and it was so enjoyable. As I spent a carefree afternoon just chatting away, I started thinking about how much I missed those afternoons living in America. Finally, we realized it was 7:00 p.m. It was still pouring, but I had to get moving to make it to my dinner. We both had to leave, so I got a trash bag from the café to protect my Louboutins from the rain and ran to catch the metro so I could make it back to the hotel and get ready for dinner. That afternoon had all been so casual and completely unplanned. We had just let go and allowed the conversation to take us anywhere and everywhere. Delightful. I find that you can only do this with certain friends here in the United States . . . not all of them. When you organize brunch with someone, there is a two- or three-hour time limit because they most likely have something else planned afterward, have to let the dogs out, or have other commitments. Sometimes, it just abruptly ends. I have been in situations where you can tell the other person is just done and ready to leave, while in France, you'd still be enjoying yourself. I guess here in the United States, it's not just restaurant servers and shopping attendants who are on the clock—it's *everyone*.

CHAPTER 15

Democracy, Schmemocracy

Back in September 2004, yours truly was fresh off the plane from France, excited about her new adventure while completely oblivious to the fact that the 2004 general election was only six weeks away. It was the 55th quadrennial presidential election—the one that saw George W. Bush get re-elected for a second term over John Kerry by a very narrow margin. A couple of weeks after my arrival, the first presidential debate took place, and I was automatically pulled into the buzz, realizing that I had to learn and understand a lot more context than I'd been taught back at school. I had the basics of how the American constitutional republic worked, but there were clearly a lot of intricacies I hadn't totally grasped. Despite a lot of similarities to the French political system, some major paradoxes in American politics were revealed to me as I experienced my first election cycle here.

In the time between that election and today, I'd like to think I've learned a lot more about the political operations of my adopted county.

But the fact remains that I'm still often left scratching my head, confused and frustrated. Both the United States and France have three branches of government: an executive branch represented by a president, a two-chambered legislative branch, and a judicial branch made up of one ultimate Supreme Court. But the similarities end there.

One of the major differences is the number of political parties in each country. I remember discussing this early on when I arrived. "What do you mean the American people only get to choose between two candidates from two major political parties?" I recalled asking one of my roommates. He explained, "Well, there are mainly Democrats and Republicans, but a few others exist that never go anywhere, like the Green Party or the Libertarians. Every election cycle, they try, but they get blocked." This was news to me. "You have a Green Party? What are Libertarians? Who are these people? I've never heard of them. I guess the foreign press doesn't really care."

I didn't understand then, and I don't understand why there can't be more parties now. Based on the diversity of ideas and opinions in this country, I would have expected at least the same number of political parties to have emerged as we have in France. The French National Assembly is comprised of 577 *députés* from thirty-nine different political parties. At the time of the 2022 French presidential election, there were nine declared candidates from nine different parties and another eight potential candidates from parties completely different from the previous nine. There ultimately was a total of twelve candidates ranging from extreme left to extreme right. Yes, union workers, communists, nationalists, and even royalists are all allowed to have candidates where I come from. It makes for a crowded campaign but offers a diversity of opinions that more accurately reflects French society—and provides a lot of entertainment, too. When I explained all this to my roommate back in 2004, he laughed and said that could never happen in the United States. It would be too hard and too expensive. The United States, it seems, is stuck with the Donkey and the Elephant.

How sad! There are more than 340 million Americans from incredibly diverse backgrounds, yet the only flavors they can choose from are chocolate and vanilla? As if strawberry, mint chocolate, rocky road, or cookie dough do not exist? And what about sorbet? This doesn't seem to register with any of the two major political parties. They seem to be happy to just come along despite polarizing ideas emerging and subsequent disagreements within their ranks. In the wake of the Civil War, the Republican Party of Abraham Lincoln, the party that allowed for emancipation, has now become more and more conservative, with religious extremists at the fray pushing their beliefs and way of life onto the moderates. Because I'm sure that's what Jesus meant when he said, "Love thy neighbor as thyself and treat others the way you want to be treated." What did Jesus intend for his followers to preach if not a message of tolerance, love, and respect? What is their *problem*? Are they not getting enough love, sex, or understanding? That decides it: More sex for the Republicans, then. That's what they need! There is a saying in French, "*mal-baisé*," which I would translate as "bad fuck." We use the term to jokingly characterize a grumpy person whose mood could be improved by more or better sex. Maybe that is the French solution to the Republican Party.

Don't think for a minute that I believe the Democrats are any better. Through the years, the Democrats have become more and more like the American version of a socialist party. Nothing quite close to the French one yet, but one that claims that social programs and initiatives from Scandinavian nations and other Western European countries should be duplicated here, the land of the free and the home of the brave. Everyone, please stop. Do you really think a program that works for the 10.35 million people living in Sweden can be duplicated exactly in a country with a population thirty-three times bigger? Have you ever heard of scale? I come from one of those economies, and it is a freaking mess. I even left, remember? Haven't you learned anything from how the French social coverage has impacted its economy? We are well known for strikes and not caring about their impact on the economy or tourism for that matter. Who was visiting Paris in December 2005, getting stuck with no subway, no train, and no flight home? Don't get me wrong, I do believe in public services and that governments are meant to provide social support networks to help lift the most vulnerable among us. No doubt about that, but not to the point of bankrupting the government. Because that's what is happening in France. No one can claim it is a successful model to be reproduced. Wake up, American progressives! Socialism doesn't work either! Instead of trying to recreate what other democracies have done, why not try to invent a model that hews closer to the American values of equality, practicality, efficiency, achievement, and success?

The Democratic Party has problems that go beyond ideology. We are talking about the same party that couldn't find a candidate who resonated with its base during arguably the most important American election of the last one hundred years, winning the 2020 presidential election by the skin of its teeth. No, the oldest, whitest, longest public-serving man was put on the docket, and only because of the highest voter turnout since 1900 was the TV reality star ousted from the top job.[1] Apparently, the Democrats couldn't bring themselves to endorse a candidate who was younger, more diverse background, more charismatic, or who didn't represent forty years of Capitol Hill establishment. Everyone within the party matching that description was unequivocally told it wasn't their turn yet. How sad, especially coming from the party that claims to stand for social, economic, and racial justice.

But just for the people living in poverty and the lower middle class, right? Again, the hypocrisy. The rich must be taxed, those "evil" people. I think, based on my income, I am what representative Alexandria Ocasio-Cortez (AOC) would call "the rich." Like many Americans, I do not come from money. I worked my ass off to get where I am, and I've always paid my taxes (even though I was not a citizen of the United States for eighteen out of the twenty years I spent here, and I didn't get a vote during that time as to how my taxes were being used, I paid them nonetheless). Apparently, the taxes I pay are not enough, and I need to pay more. How much more, though? I do not own a private jet or a yacht; unfortunately, I can't afford them. If I were to get legally married to my husband, which I am not today, the IRS would take my full gross income. Any chance one of them understands that there is a big difference between a household making six figures and one making seven or more a year? Change the freaking threshold, simplify the tax code, and let's be done with this. How hypocritical—social justice and equality, but not for everyone. If Republicans need more sex, what do Democrats need? Better candidates, more common-sense platforms, and more guts!

---

[1] Hannah Hartig, Andrew Daniller, Scott Keeter, and Ted Van Green, "Voter Turnout 2018–2022," Pew Research Center, July 12, 2023, https://www.pewresearch.org/politics/2023/07/12/voter-turnout-2018-2022/.

Let's move on to the topic of the presidential election and its voting process. Despite having the universal right to vote as provided by the US Constitution, doing so has many complications. There are primaries and caucuses (what are those again?) throughout the fifty states, followed by the general election on the first Tuesday of November. Then, the Electoral College votes in early December, the election is certified sometime thereafter, and the winning candidate is inaugurated in January on the day of my birthday. This circus happens every four years and lasts around two years. It is as if campaigning is the favorite pastime of American politicians.

The Republican and Democratic primaries start as soon as six months before the parties' respective conventions, during which their presidential tickets are officially endorsed. However, announcing your candidacy and running for those positions start as early as fifteen months before the primary. This concept was completely unknown to me when I arrived in the United States, as it is nonexistent in the French electoral process. It is certainly exhausting. During the primaries, the same messages are being communicated again and again, and whoever finally receives the endorsement seems to come down to whoever has been able to keep their skeletons in the closet. Anyone with dirt they can't conceal gets washed out: if they've smoked pot, had an affair, sexually harassed women (although sometimes they become president anyway), hidden emails... The list of indiscretions goes on. The winner is usually the candidate with the fewest secrets, who made the fewest gaffes. What about their platforms, you might ask? This is just secondary. After all, what is more important: What the candidate wants to accomplish or whether they behaved properly according to public opinion?

The primary debates are easily the best part of the election process in America. Each side has a bunch of candidates all on one stage, all talking over each other and strategically ganging up on one another to increase their chances. What a show! It is quite entertaining, and despite the American people being less inclined to watch presidential debates during the primaries, I have always been a fervent audience—trying to thrash through the BS and make sense of their platforms. To my dismay, it always turns out to be more of a pissing contest. It might be worth thinking about bringing this bizarre display behind closed doors. But then, the TV broadcasters would miss their opportunity to secure better ratings. In all honesty, for the last couple of presidential election cycles, French political parties, mainly the major ones, have started engaging in the same type of primaries as in the United States. They are even copying the debate model and televising all those candidates on national TV, allowing them to make their case as to why they should be their party's nominee. They're messy and laughable. This is one American influence on the French political process I do not endorse.

After the primary circus ends, the general election circus gets in motion. Everyone gets up on the first Tuesday of November and goes to stand in line to vote. I will not touch on how absentee ballots work, thank you very much. There are too many variables per state. It's not even funny. When I first learned how the US general election worked back in 2004, my first reaction was, "Excuse me, but people have to go vote on *what* day? Don't most people *work* on Tuesdays?" This came as a major surprise, even though the United States is not the only country that holds general elections on a weekday. Many others, including Canada, Denmark, Indonesia, the Netherlands, the

Philippines, South Korea, and the United Kingdom, do as well. However, in a country where there is no extensive social coverage, and many people have multiple jobs to make ends meet, you would think that they'd have picked a more convenient day. (Yes, I can hear you already—the United States does also have early voting for two weeks leading up to election day that is much less restrictive and helps ease some of these problems—but maybe you wouldn't need it if it was at a more convenient time and you had dedicated voter polling stations.) As my US friends have had to explain to me time and time again, this is a historical conundrum that would require changing a law from 1845, back when most of the country were farmers and nine-to-five jobs didn't exist yet. By November, the harvest was completed, and the harsh winter hadn't started yet. Most people went to church on Sunday, traveled from their rural homes to polling stations on Monday, and then voted on Tuesday so they could be home by Wednesday for market day. All this makes sense. But why choose the first Tuesday in November? With the development of the Morse telegraph, Congress didn't want one state election to be unduly influenced by the others, so they passed a law mandating a uniform national electoral day, still allowing a thirty-four-day period for states to select their presidential electors to travel to DC for the Electoral College to elect the president on the first Wednesday of December.

Fast-forward 175 years to the adoption of the internet, and you would think Congress might regroup and decide that it might be time to move the general election to a more suitable day of the week. Or even explore a more reliable way to digitize voting. We keep hearing about ballot fraud, missing ballots, or incorrectly filled ballots. It is as if having electronic voting machines is causing more harm than the good, old-fashioned paper method. The other issue is that ballots all include a significant number of confusing propositions to vote for or against on the same day. Of course, why would you keep it simple? Let's confuse the heck out of everyone so it is more difficult to pick the candidate you intend to vote for. As much as we are sophisticated human beings, there are still things we are better at doing one at a time. Maybe the current Congress could get more attuned to the innovation of their time. Just a thought—and a French one, for that matter!

France still uses paper ballots for most elections. That's right, we still head to our designated polling stations, hosted at public schools, on a Sunday, to hide behind a curtain, put a little piece of paper in two sealed envelopes, and drop them into an urn while a voting volunteer says: "*A voté!*" But it is fast evolving. I had the chance to vote in the parliamentary elections via the internet for the first time this year. Any chance the United States could catch up? (Again, I can hear you—yes, you are ahead of France on the voting machine front. It's still paper, but it is digitized so it can be counted faster. You'd be correct; France still manually counts the votes with volunteers after the polling stations close!) The most innovative country seems to be delaying adopting technology to streamline voting, but why? You can do pretty much everything else related to federal administrative tasks online. What's the catch? Fraud? Hacking? Let me take a guess: It would allow for easier voting registration, more stringent identification, and a clearer and more streamlined process. Additionally, people would not have to take a day off from work or stand in never-ending lines to vote. Can you believe it? Such a nice thought.

Or it might just be because no election is that simple. French people only get to vote on one thing at a time. Every time American people are being asked to vote, they have to make decisions on a multitude of positions and propositions . . . sometimes up to 20-25 . . . president, governor, lieutenant-governor, congress positions, state congress positions, railroad commissioners, mayors, city councils, school boards, prop A, prop B, . . . prop Z! If you want to thoroughly vote, you are expected to do a significant amount of research on all candidates and propositions. Scratch of the head! How are people supposed to find the appropriate amount of time to read on all those and make an educated decision? And are we sure that most people, including myself, are the best qualified to elect a railroad commissioner? What does this role entail anyway? Apparently, in Texas, it is in charge of all the oil and gas regulations, coal and uranium mining operations, and pipelines. I thought this person was mainly in charge of "choo choo" trains and the railroads but not any longer. All of those were transferred to other agencies in 2005. And I just made my point! Ludicrous—how is anybody supposed to learn, keep up, and educate themselves ahead of an election? Most people work, and some of them have multiple jobs. You wonder why people vote along party lines. I would, or I would at least try to balance my votes—top jobs I understand, this way, and then to balance it, some of the other jobs—the other way! Not a great look or outcome, either. Can't really get anything done anyway, but at least I would be hedging my bets! Election Day 2004 is a little blurry and has faded in my memory. However, Election Day 2016 is as clear as can be. I remember exactly where I was, who I was with, and what occurred. I was alone in a hotel room in Boston, lying in bed with the TV on. The results started coming in, and as more and more states came back with Trump leading, I fell asleep thinking I already knew who'd won. When I finally woke up, it was a few minutes before the final call, and you all know the outcome. What was unbelievable was that the candidate who'd won the popular vote was not the one declared the winner. All because of the Electoral College. I still can't believe that this institution exists. Back in 2004, my first reaction to learning about it was, "What the heck is this? Please explain why one person's vote doesn't count for one vote in the total count. What is this about?" Despite universal suffrage, I discovered that US presidential elections are indirect, meaning citizens vote for electors of the Electoral College, who then go on and vote for the president. Historical facts for you: Congress initially created this to avoid directly voting for the president and protect the separation of powers, which makes total sense. However, the delegates quickly acknowledged that a popular vote would make more sense. But at that point in time, it was too late to secure consensus from the South—take a guess why. In 1787, the model was approved and, despite a few changes since then, has remained in place.

Why keep it? Each citizen's choice should count as much as any other's. Shouldn't this be one of the pillars of democracy? Every four years, the suspense builds up—who will win the Electoral College vote, and who will win the popular vote? But don't be fooled, it has happened several times in history, and it will most likely happen again—the president of the United States will not be the winner of the popular vote, and their opponent will have to acknowledge defeat, lick their wounds, and continue on with a political career knowing that most of the country really wanted them to govern. Tough luck! And that is how, every four years, the circus finally ends: with a country usually divided, sometimes upset, and me still scratching my head while the inauguration gets on its way.

I must sound sarcastic or even cynical, but coming from a country where the right to vote is engrained in you as early as elementary school through civics classes, where registering to vote is as easy as showing up at city hall, and where the act of voting is considered a civic duty, a badge of honor, or an expression of your opinion, how can this be? Despite its diversity, the United States is locked into a two-party system, preventing others from emerging and providing alternative ideologies, platforms, and solutions. Despite advocating for democracy around the world, America's own voting system has not grown along with time and innovation. Despite its belief in righteousness and public service, lobbyists and money win elections, not platforms or public service achievements.

Fast-forward to seventeen years later: it's 2021, and I have now been through five US presidential election cycles, including three Democratic and two Republican wins. I saw the first African American president sworn in, the first woman nominated as a candidate for a major party lose, a reality TV star make it to the top spot, and the oldest sitting president in history take on the job. I am also way better informed on the process and its history.

So, should I consider becoming an active participant in the circus? I'm not sure it would be good for my mental health. Can you see this wild French lady all up in arms, trying to make a change by considering a career in politics? Based on my family history, it would make sense, but it might not be a good idea—it got my grandpa sent to his death in a Russian gulag, after all! By now, readers, you might have guessed that with my directness, lack of diplomacy—and I'll even add lack of patience—I would make the worst political operator. But if I ever were asked to serve by POTUS, FLOTUS, SCOTUS, SCHMOTUS, then who would I be to refuse?

CHAPTER 16

Puritans in Porn Star Clothing

Not long after I moved from France, I broke up with my French boyfriend since our long-distance love only lasted about a month—remember? At that point, I started dating one of my roommates, an American guy. This was my first romantic experience with an American, and I found myself pretty surprised when that first night came along. You know what I am talking about. First base, second base, third base, and home plate—here we come! The foreplay was fine, but when we finally got into it, I just remember lying there and thinking, *This is not how it is supposed to be done! Take a chill pill, man! Who taught you about the deed, and where did you get that fucking like a rabbit is the way to go? What is going on? Did I end up in my own porn movie or something?* The pace he set was unsustainable, and I'm not sure how he didn't realize that this could *not* have been fun or felt good for me. No pleasure could come out of the way he was going about things. Couldn't he just tell? Where was this coming from?

At this point, of course, I hadn't actually said anything to him and was mostly just waiting for it to be over. I had a completely internal conversation in my own head and was crossing my fingers—though obviously not my legs—that this would be over sooner rather than later. Finally, it came to an end. Now it was time to try and discuss what had just happened. Here I was, tiptoeing around the topic, trying as nicely as possible to tell a man four years older than me that it was great but that maybe next time we could try something else. Me taking the lead, for example, so I could show him what I liked (and how to do it properly). The good news is that he ended up being very gracious about it and open to taking my lead. I think I got lucky, as it turned into a teaching relationship, and he was a fast learner. But those jackrabbit moves would still come back once in a while, and I'd be thinking, *Not again, please, no, no, no; this is not a porn movie! I like to watch but I really do not need to recreate this in my own bed!*

My guess is that whatever "birds-and-the-bees" talk he got from his parents, sure didn't include a part about "Now let me tell you a bit more about how making love can be." He came from a very Irish-Catholic family, and I couldn't imagine his mom or dad, such kind people, sitting any of their kids down and having that kind of conversation. I might be wrong, but from talking to other American friends, I doubt sex is being discussed in most American families. Certainly not at school during sex education. My understanding is that sex education in America is pretty basic: this is a woman's body, this is a man's body, and this is how you make babies. As for how you avoid ending up with a baby or how you might make love with someone when you don't intend to make a baby at all, that is not being talked about in every school, is it?

Growing up in France, I remember having two sex education classes in school. In one class, I ended up being called to the front to demonstrate how to put a condom on a banana—lucky me! In France, we also seem to experience sexuality and discuss it with our friends and parents a bit more easily. I kissed my first boyfriend at five, and I would hide during recess in elementary school to practice kissing with my girlfriends to be ready to kiss boys. We would fake making love during middle school to be ready for our first time. I brought up the topic with my mom when I was twelve. It seems like that conversation literally just happened. I can still see myself in the car: We had just gone grocery shopping, and I raised the topic, telling her I was starting to think about sex, when I would be ready for it, and what I needed to know about it. I don't know if my mom was uncomfortable, though I highly doubt it, as she doesn't get uncomfortable that easily (a family trait). By the time we got home twenty minutes later, my initial questions were answered, from how I would know whether I was ready to protecting myself—not just with contraception but also physically and emotionally—to understanding that sex is part of a healthy relationship and life in general. It turned more into a discussion about self-preservation instead of solely a conversation about sex. My mom felt more compelled to make sure I would be safe with potential sex partners than to give me tips for how to make love to someone. In hindsight, I totally get it, and some of the things she told me definitely stuck with me: Don't put yourself in a situation where you lose control; always be aware of your surroundings, especially at night; make sure you are not being followed. I guess people would say I was very mature and maybe even sexually mature and sexually focused for my age. It might be because of the culture and family I grew up with. Sex was never portrayed to me as something bad or sinful for that matter, and all the talks and silly behaviors helped me be prepared to have a healthy sexual life. But I can't claim or confirm that this is the norm in France either. I do think that French people talk about it more freely, especially between friends, and I do believe families might be more open about it, too. The sexual culture of the French has been exported by way of French kissing, *ménage à trois*, affairs, and lovers. You could say our reputation precedes us!

What has been baffling since living here in the United States is hearing what people are teaching kids about sex and contraception. How many times have I heard about "the pullout method" or abstinence being used for birth control? How can people think teenage kids with their hormones going crazy will not be tempted to experiment with their sexuality? And then you experience a situation with the pullout method, and that would have never happened with a French guy . . .

I dated a guy in San Francisco back in 2009. I met him on Memorial Day during carnival weekend and we went on a couple of dates afterward. On one of those dates, maybe the last one, we met for dinner at a sushi place close to my apartment, and then he walked me home. I invited him over, and the game started. First base, second and third base, and then the awkward moment arrived—the one during which this French girl expected the guy to pull out a condom. In this case, I had to stop the guy and ask whether he had a condom. He looked at me and just said, "I don't like how it feels, so I would prefer not to use one." I stopped him again and said, "Sorry, there is no deed without a condom." Again, I was baffled. I barely knew him, and he barely knew me. We hadn't exchanged medical records, nor did I know where he had been putting his dick. There is no way I was taking a risk or getting pregnant. Apparently, the guy didn't care—about sexually transmitted infections, pregnancy, or whatever. All he cared about was the feeling of a condom on his penis. Un-fucking-believable! No guy in France would assume that it was okay to have sex for the first time without a condom! It never happened to me back home, and I have been sexually active since I was fifteen, for heaven's sake!

When I moved to the United States, I had a preconceived notion of sex based on the movies I watched growing up. I thought everyone here was having sex, that Americans were great lovers and kissers, and that it was such a romantic culture. (Americans do make great rom-coms, which screwed up my expectations of romance, love, and relationships—thank you very much!) Pretty soon after I moved here, I realized none of this was real. Most people barely talk about sex; it can even be considered a shameful thing. Strangely, people seem to have sex with multiple people at the same time in the game called "dating." And the United States has the biggest porn industry in the world! By the way, France is only number five on that list.

I had also developed a bit of a skewed perception of what dating in the United States would be like from watching *Sex and the City*. I am from the generation who grew up with the HBO show, and I guess I took to heart the fantasy of chatting over brunch with your best girlfriends about your fun, breezy romances and sexual escapades. So, when I landed, I quickly realized there were many strange dating games being played, and the country was a bit more conservative about sex than Carrie, Miranda, Charlotte, and Samantha would have had me believe. Those four women living the New York City life represented all women on the sex spectrum for me, from free-for-all

Samantha to playing hard-to-get Charlotte. I ended up identifying somewhere in the middle. Fine, I wanted to be Carrie! Not just for the relationships and the sex but for those shoes, ladies! (I have my Louboutins, but no Manolos for me—yet!)

I remember discussing sex with one of my best friends, an American, and discovering that she never had one-night stands (maybe once on vacation) and that she would actually wait three to four months before sleeping with any of her dates. My head was spinning, and I was thinking, *Oh gosh, I would never have been able to wait that long . . . please do not judge me!* I felt clueless about how to play this dating game in America, and instead of having a group of supportive friends to chat about it with at brunch, I faced a lot of judgment. Sometimes the judgments were unspoken because no one would talk about sex that openly here. It took more than thirteen years for my friend to open up about sex and have this conversation with me about what is really important in relationships. For me, sex is important for a healthy relationship, but it's not a priority for her. We are all different, and we were all raised differently, but I was still puzzled that it took so long for us to have such a deep and important discussion.

As a result, I felt it was harder for me to have sex in America during my short dating life. I must have been too honest about my background, my education, and my work—which apparently was quite unattractive to American men. Since I didn't know how to play the hard-to-get game, it was a double whammy for me. My available pool of interested men became way smaller. Less dating meant less sex for me. It had felt much easier back home to just go out with someone and get some. I took a tally before and after I moved to the United States, and somehow, I was more successful back home than here. Even when

I went home after I had moved, I could call an ex, and we would hang out, go out, and have fun for the short time I was back. No big deal. A nice evening of catching up would naturally turn into something more with no awkward moments, no pain on either side, just two consenting adults enjoying life and having a good time. Nothing ever really felt that way during my five years of dating in the United States. Sex always felt like a big deal. There was always a lot of pressure around dating and having a good time. There were many awkward moments due to me being direct and honest, which men often found threatening or intimidating. Then, in other situations, I would find myself needing to protect myself and stand my ground. It was exhausting in hindsight. What was I going to do anyway, pretend for a full evening, and then what? Pretend for the rest of the time? Great way to start an honest relationship! How stupid would that be? Overall, I was quite deflated by my dating experience in America. I was just not able to live the Carrie life.

But it's not just American TV and movies that are oversexed compared to the way people act in real life—it's the clothing, too. In fact, some people's dress code seems awfully in contradiction with their religious beliefs. Walking the streets of Miami or in line at Victoria's Secret in Texas, I've seen some women pretty much walking with everything and anything showing. I remember my first Halloween in San Francisco, right after I had moved from Seattle, and feeling completely out of step with the spirit of wearing the appropriate costume for that night. As some friends and I went bar hopping, I discovered this was the one night of the year during which women would wear the least amount of clothing, showing as much skin as possible under the veil of a Halloween costume. Yes, I am being a bit of a prude, and my costume that year didn't fit the theme at all—too much coverage for the city—but unfortunately, between my grandma and my mom, I was raised to dress sexy but properly—no boob or butt cheek showing at any time. Overall, I would say good for those women to feel empowered and confident enough to pull off those revealing outfits. I guess I was raised a bit differently: Keep a slight veil of mystery, my grandma would say! Am I being judgmental? Maybe. A little contradictory? Possibly. I think there is still a difference between dressing sexy and showing some skin versus just having your woman attributes out there for the showing. You might say I have double standards, but I seriously wonder whether there is a contradiction between underdressing and one's religious beliefs and how it reconciles with the Puritans coming to America over four hundred years ago with their strict ideas about modesty and decency. Now it seems the country has overcorrected to the other extreme of skin display and porn.

Regardless of what young women are wearing or how much skin they are showing, the contradiction in American sexuality that I will never be able to reconcile is the difference in how men's and women's sexualities are treated here. Men are allowed to have sex and do essentially whatever they please sexually—especially before marriage—but if a woman does the same, she is a slut! *Excuse me?* And in families, American fathers are more likely to be overprotective of their daughters when they begin dating, while the sons, of course, get more leniency. A girl shouldn't have sex before marriage, but a boy is more than allowed to do so. It is even expected. Don't get me wrong—French dads are as protective of their daughters, but I think they might be a bit more realistic about it and would rather their daughters be safe than sorry. They'd rather talk to their daughters about contraception and sexual assault than pretend they don't need to know how to protect themselves or don't have any sexuality of their own. Dads might not want to know about their daughters' adventures, but they are ready and available if anything happens. My dad told me straight up he would kill the guy if I was ever raped and that he had no problem going to prison for it. But he never told me not to have sex or wait until I got married either.

I do not know where it leaves us in the United States. Despite the contradictory fashion statements and surprising dating games, it feels as if the country overall has not come out of its Puritan past and adjusted to its evolving society. It's almost as if every aspect of the culture in the United States is always underpinned—sometimes obviously and sometimes invisibly—by religious ideology. This aspect is much more prevalent in everyday life than it is in France, where the culture is more secular in general. It almost feels like, despite being the land of the free, the United States might not be as accepting as France when it comes to certain areas of life.

CHAPTER 17

So, Which Box Do I Check?

When it comes to the matter of race, I need to do better. I have tried to use my voice to support those who have historically been marginalized and will continue doing so every single day through actions and mindfulness.

When I first landed in the United States and got to UW, they asked me to fill in some paperwork. The forms I received included a question about what my "race" was. I genuinely didn't know what to answer. Nobody had ever asked me that in twenty-two years in France, no school or government or job application. In fact, the French government does not collect information on the racial makeup of its population. Somebody had to explain to me what "Caucasian" meant. I was like, "What do you mean I'm Caucasian?" I guess I understood the region of the world that the word was referring to, but it felt wrong. Yes, I am White European. But I'm actually a big blend—remember, not a coffee blend, but still? I'm not really French.

I'm a first-generation born and raised in France. My mom is from North Africa, and my dad is from Eastern Europe. Why did I have to pick a box? I guess I am awfully fair-skinned, and most people think I am awfully white, so fine, I ended up picking the White/Caucasian box. To this day, I do believe that trying to fit people into boxes or categories is part of the problem. People are more fluid in terms of what they identify with, and having to pick a box somehow puts everyone in some sort of competitive situation. Which box is better?

By the way, do you know where the term "Caucasian" comes from? It was legally adopted by the United States in the eighteenth century. German anthropologist, Johann Blumenbach, first used the term for a derogatory system of racial classification after a visit to the Caucasus mountains.[1] He had set out to create a system of labels for different races, and he became enamored with the appearance of the people there and determined that they had an ideal form of beauty. From then on, in his research and studies on racial anthropology, he would refer to Caucasians as those with European ancestry. Perhaps it's time to retire this classification and move to something closer to reality such as country of origin or ancestry.

When I first started writing this book, I didn't think it was my place to write anything about the discourse surrounding race, racism, and equality in the United States, despite my complete puzzlement at all that continues to occur year after year. Though I am a mix of two completely different backgrounds—Sephardic Jew from North Africa on my mom's side and Russian Orthodox from Eastern Europe on my

---

[1] "Where Does the Word Caucasian Come From?" *Context Travel*, June 15, 2022, https://www.contexttravel.com/blog/articles/where-does-the-word-caucasian-come-from; Yolanda Moses, "Why Do We Keep Using the Word 'Caucasian'?" *SAPIENS Newsletter*, February 1, 2017, https://www.sapiens.org/culture/caucasian-terminology-origin/.

dad's side—I am still as white as I can be. But after the events of 2020, I have reached a point where I just can't comprehend how, after all these years, people can still act with such extreme prejudice toward people of other skin color, religion, or sexual orientation.

First, I'd love for all of us to understand that although, because of social constructions, we may identify as different races, genetically we are only *one human species*—one humankind. We all bleed red, we all have the same genetic materials, we all have the same anatomy, and we all come with our own talents. To illustrate that point, let's take a familiar comparison: There is only one species we call canine. However, they come in all shapes and sizes—Labradors, Havanese, bulldogs, German shepherds, and mutts. If you were to listen to my husband, he would compare me to a French bulldog—after all, I am French, and they are known for being stubborn, difficult to train, but affectionate, according to the American Kennel Club. That is when I start comparing him to an English bulldog (yes, he is English) as they are grumpy, and their gait screams, "I am in charge," despite them just wanting to curl on your lap!

Why can we see the cuteness in all those shapes and forms but can't see that in each other's differences? Why is it difficult to keep that in mind? Why is it so easy to be afraid of people who look different from us? And what on earth do the people who harm those who are different from them have in mind when they are carrying out such unacceptable actions? How does a police officer come to think that putting his knee on someone's neck is ever appropriate? How have we created a culture where he feels justified in this behavior, especially when the man in question is obviously in distress? You can go back to any of the myriad incidents of this kind and wonder the same. Have we lost the belief that every life is precious and priceless? No matter which religion you follow, or even if you don't follow any, most moral frameworks agree that every human life is sacred.

How can we stop expending more energy on divisive debate than we do on taking action? How can we, as a society, help break the destructive cycle we are in? Our understanding of racial bias should have been improved by now. The Civil Rights Movement is more than sixty years old, and continued immigration has only brought more diversity to this country. Yet, instead of creating more room for empathy and mutual understanding, these developments seem to have triggered a reactionary ideology in which too many people view the increasing diversity of the United States as a threat to their own economic and moral security. And the politics surrounding these issues are not helping. .

I was having a conversation with my dear friend recently. He's a former boss who has become a good friend. We got to talking about the idea of race and the ways it affects our experiences in America. I was writing an article about it on LinkedIn and needed someone who could give me unfiltered feedback about the piece. You see, he is White, and his wife is African American; their children are multiracial. In addition to getting his take on my writing, I also wanted to check in on him and his family with everything that was going on during the spring of 2020. He and I are both problem-solvers at heart, so once we got started talking about the piece, we ended up discussing what could be done to change things, too.

Here are some of the ideas we identified as capable of helping to make a change. Each action below, if taken alone, would not be sufficient. Only a combination of these actions—and more—could stand a hope of making a difference.

1. EARLY EDUCATION

We have to start by educating children. Nobody is born to hate. We can influence generations upon generations by ensuring we teach both public- and private-school children not just tolerance of but appreciation for our differences. This would involve incorporating mandatory lessons on American and world history, religion, art, and culture that demonstrate the value of our diversity as a people. Somewhat more challengingly, this objective would also require biology curriculums to clearly instruct the next generations on the difference between the scientific reality of species and the sociocultural concept of race, so they will grow up understanding that despite our differences, we are all humankind.

To prevent the formation of prejudices, it is also essential that children are socialized with people outside of their own culture and socioeconomic background as early as possible. To this end, we need to push for more school field trips early on to expose children to more and different facets of humanity. When I was twelve years old, attending middle school back in France, our class took a trip to Greece to learn more about the history of democracy as well as Greek mythology. It was not that far from home, but the trip served to open us all up to new ideas and a different culture. The Greek people ate different food and looked somewhat different from most of us, but the experience felt safe, and we were excited to learn more—especially because it allowed us to be away from our parents! A lot of us even caught the travel bug from this trip, and since then, we've been continuing to discover the world outside our place of birth, a habit that I believe brings with it a higher level of tolerance and understanding of others. It is not a guarantee, but it's certainly a good start. It is time to create the most tolerant and open generation of its kind!

2. TRAINING (A.K.A. CONTINUING EDUCATION)

It's not just American children who have much to learn about other people and the greater world around them. Adults are not a lost cause when it comes to education (or reeducation, as the case may be) about implicit bias, prejudice, and stereotypes. I see that two adult populations most in need of training on matters of diversity and cultural differences are the general public and law enforcement.

General Public

It has been clearly established by the events and discourse of the past few years that, no matter how accepting and educated they are, most Americans still hold biases against members of the population who are unlike them in one or more respects: race, gender, socioeconomic status, religion, and so on. Many of these biases are unconscious—I know for a fact that I still hold many of them myself without even noticing—and without deliberate thought and training, these biases will continue to go unexamined, where they can continue to do harm to members of our community. I experience privileges because of my identity as a White cis woman, but most of us have one or more identities that afford us power and privilege that we take for granted. As a result, most of us can do better when it comes to learning to recognize our own privilege, thus making visible the ways those who are not like us are minimized or denied that same power. This applies in both our personal and professional lives. Why not incorporate required yearly training both in higher education as well as in workplaces to remind us not to be ignorant of lives and perspectives other than our own? What about turning those trainings into certificates or credits related to gaining knowledge about others instead of the dreaded compulsory HR training? The more credits you accrue, the more rewards you can choose from. Companies already do this for wellness, so why not for diversity and inclusion? Some might say it's ridiculous to resort to incentivizing ourselves to develop empathy, and I would not disagree. But what we're doing now isn't working, so what do we have to lose?

Law Enforcement

This is where I think I am biased by my European upbringing. Most police forces in Western Europe are trained to de-escalate situations, not "neutralize" perceived "threats" by escalating confrontations. Law enforcement training in France puts an emphasis on the police's role as community servants. By contrast, in the United States, police are meant to "serve and protect"; the fact that in 2021, police in the United States shot and killed 1,048 people[2] seems to undermine that clever motto. In France, the number of police fatalities in 2021 was fifty-two,[3] and it was *a record-high year.* Even controlling for the difference in population between the two countries, the amount of police violence in America is staggering.

---

[2] "Number of People Shot to Death by the Police in the United States from 2017 to 2024*, by Race," Statista Research Department, March 11, 2024, https://www.statista.com/statistics/585152/people-shot-to-death-by-us-police-by-race/.
[3] "Annual Number of Deaths Linked to Police Intervention in France between 2010 and 2022," Statista Research Department, March 11, 2024, https://www.statista.com/statistics/1396712/number-police-related-deaths-france/#:~:text=In%20France%2C%20the%20number%20of,deaths%20were%20recorded%20in%202021.

While the law enforcement rhetoric may look similar in both France and America, the difference in fatalities likely comes down to the strict way in which law enforcement's use of lethal force is regulated in France, creating an emphasis on nonlethal tactics in police training. Officers are taught to remain calm and try to talk with the subject, to use their presence as a deterrent as opposed to relying on action to deter, and not to pull their firearms until the situation meets the requirements established by the nationwide legal restrictions on the use of lethal force by police. It has only been since 2017, when these restrictions were loosened, that French deaths by police violence have begun to rise (hence that record-high 2021 statistic).[4] However, overall, law enforcement in France is less reliant on firearms. Municipal police, the local law enforcement in French towns and cities, often do not carry guns at all (though the French National Police and the National Gendarmerie, roughly equivalent to the US National Guard, typically do). It is a completely different mindset. French police are largely trained to protect and serve their communities and, as a result, don't suffer from the same militarization as their American counterparts. Adopting this kind of community-focused training, emphasizing de-escalation techniques and the use of nonlethal force is critical to staving off the injustice people, especially Black people, suffer at the hands of police in America, and this training should start immediately.

---

[4] Claudia Lauer and Alanna Durkin Richer, "Shooting in France Shows US Is Not Alone in Struggles with Racism, Police Brutality," *AP News*, July 1, 2023, https://apnews.com/article/paris-police-teen-killing-george-floyd-61db9ba68b874d3b02bfcbf51da18a1a.

3. CRIMINAL JUSTICE REFORM

I must admit that this is the subject on this list about which I am least knowledgeable. However, it is my understanding that there is a disproportionate number of people of color incarcerated in American prisons when compared to the makeup of the general population. And let me be clear: Black people are disproportionately targeted. So much for following the Constitution of the United States—the Fourteenth Amendment, if I recall properly! What guidelines are the judiciary bench following? If two people come before your court accused of the same transgression, with the same prior background, and one is White while the other is Black, what is causing you to incarcerate one but not the other or to give one a longer sentence than the other? Based on what? I doubt it has anything to do with the law. This is another example of the effects of implicit bias against others for their differences.

If judges were able to take on their cases devoid of these biases, the appropriate course of action would be to incarcerate White people and people of color at similar rates for comparable prison terms. But they clearly can't. What the solution is to this structural discrimination, I'm not entirely sure. But according to the Brennan Center for Justice, changing required sentences for first-time misdemeanors and reducing incarceration for nonviolent offenses across the board would hopefully solve part of the problem.[5] Increasing the budget for quality public defense representation would also help close the gap for those who are unable to afford to retain their own legal defense. Mandating

---

[5] Jessica Eaglin and Danyelle Solomon, "Reducing Racial and Ethnic Disparities in Jails," Brennan Center, June 25, 2015, https://www.brennancenter.org/our-work/policy-solutions/reducing-racial-and-ethnic-disparities-jails#:~:text=This%20report%2C%20which%20relies%20on,to%20prioritize%20serious%20and%20violent.

training to reduce bias in judges and other criminal justice professionals would be a natural step toward restoring balance. Finally, I believe that educating children about diversity and socializing them outside of their communities might ensure this problem lessens over time as older judges retire and younger judges take their places.

4. STOP USING THE TERM "RACE"

I know this sounds silly, but why can't we stop using the word "race"? Could we instead talk about each person as part of the human race, but acknowledge that they all have different backgrounds? Will the terms used to talk about race eventually become obsolete as more and more people comingle? What should we call the blended majority that will eventually emerge? I refuse to call it "mixed race." This is inaccurate. In botany, it would be called hybrid, and in zoology, crossbreed. But I don't think any of those are good candidates. Maybe we should just go with "blends." I am one of them. New terms will inevitably develop as society progresses, and I hope we keep the following in mind—we are all a medley of different backgrounds, after all, and that is what makes our world so rich with cultures, flavors, perspectives, and traditions.

5. INCLUSIVE POLITICS

American politics has reached a tipping point—the discourse has become so divisive that nothing gets done for the good of the people. I have been following American politics for the last twenty years. It was the least I could do, as this country allowed me to study and begin a career and life here. I have watched as the political rhetoric has become worse and worse. By the way, the blame for this falls on both sides of the aisle. No party is better than the other at this point. I propose we try something new:

Time to Kick the Two-Party System Down the Drain.

As I discussed in Chapter 15, a lack of money and cronies should not prevent the formation of new political parties from being formed, especially more centrist ones. In French presidential elections, we always start with somewhere around fifteen candidates from fifteen different parties and end up selecting a president from the two front-runners after the results of a first-round election. It has definitely created some interesting and scary situations in the past, but at least every possible voice was represented. The Green Party and Libertarians have tried to go all the way in the past to no avail in America. It's time to take a chance and show what real politics can be if we allow for more than two voices.

Time for Campaign Reform.

No more lobbyists and no more making it all about who raises the most money. All campaign fundraising should be capped, forcing candidates to run based on the merit of their policies and not who can pay for the most ads. That is absolutely ridiculous! Think about all the money spent that could have been better used to solve certain social issues instead of electing candidates who *say* they care about those issues.

Time to Shock the Political Scene.

The two items mentioned earlier will take time to implement, no doubt. So, what is there to do? In the last election cycle, I was really hoping for a shockwave with an unexpected ticket in November's election. You want to heal the country, show that the parties can work together, get things done, and make society better?

How unexpected would it have been to allow for some new-blood leadership to bring moderate Democrats and Republicans with different views, genders, backgrounds, and ethnicities on one ticket? How about that for a disrupter! What better way to have encouraged Never-Trump Republicans to turn up at the polls and offset the Democrats who, dismayed by Biden's first-term performance, would inevitably sit this election out or decide to lean the other way?

It's not even an unreasonable suggestion. In fact, this concept is called a "unity ticket," and it's a strategy often employed to unite a country during times of political unrest. Both Brazil and Taiwan have elected presidents running on unity tickets in the last ten years. They've never been a particularly effective strategy in the United States since the last time one won the presidency was 1864. Notably, though, that president was Abraham Lincoln. So maybe it's just a question of how much social unrest Americans will tolerate before they consider a split presidential ticket? Why not now? The time is now!

CHAPTER 18

The Ugly Truth about Cursing

All right let's get this out of the way from the start: We have a lot of cuss words in France, and we do curse a lot. After twenty years of "research," I think cursing in France might be even worse than in the United States. Fluency in curse words comes a little later in life for French people because you don't *ever* do it in front of your parents or your teachers at school. If my parents had heard me use a curse word, it would've been considered extremely disrespectful, and I would have been scolded and grounded. My family was quite proper on this. Some small words were allowed as I grew a bit older: *merde* ("crap/shit"), *fais chier* ("it's f-ing annoying"), or *pourri* ("that is crap"). Most of these words are not meant to insult people, so in France, our parents cut us some slack for using them as teenagers.

By the time I turned eighteen, my playground practice had provided a robust skillset. Bear in mind that we have a variety of words with their own degree of spiciness for everything and anything! So

I was already predisposed to cursing, and then I watched a lot of American movies growing up where actors and actresses were walking around saying, "fuck this" and "fuck that." *Score!* You think to yourself. *This is a cursing country, and I am going to fit right in.*

Once I landed, I quickly realized—once again—that movies weren't reality. Nor was the United States playing by the same rules as in France. As a student, I think things were a little looser, especially outside of school with my friends. Some foul language would fly around on a regular basis. But once I transitioned into the workforce, I discovered that one curse word in the workplace can lead to a bad performance review . . .

It took me quite some time to develop my American foul language. In fact, when I landed, it was not very extensive. I didn't even know what "the C-word" meant (by the way, in France, this is the least offensive word for women and usually means being stupid, so I quickly had to learn the subtleties of the word here in the United States). I mainly knew "fuck," "asshole," and "bitch." I had to learn all the shades of insulting someone—from stupid (*stupide*) to bitch (*salope*) to whore (*putain*) to c... (*conne*) or dick (*connard*) to asshole (*trou du cul*) to motherfucker (*connard/couillon*). Cursing is like any other language: Until you live in the country and immerse yourself in the language, you do not know all the wonderful ways to express yourself to people or for *them* to express themselves to *you*.

Even now, I am sure I still don't even know the full spectrum. For extra credit, you can also add in British English words like "twat" or the full-on cursing expressions that they absolutely do not teach you at school (e.g., "son of a bitch"). You can imagine how out of my depth I was when I landed in Seattle as a student. At least I got a few years to learn it all before getting into the workforce and realizing that there was no foul language allowed at the staff level, even though some partners would curse right and left. But you know how it is: Everything's different at the top of the food chain. No shit!

Out of all the curse words I learned to use in English, I really took to the f-bomb. I guess I couldn't let it go. I had to keep the stereotype going after learning it from the silver screen. It is as if the English created a perfect word that can be easily inserted in every possible sentence—fuck this, fuck that. We do not have an easy f-bomb in France. The closest I can think of is *putain*, and it doesn't even come close to being as versatile as "fuck!" Do you think "fuck" is the best-known word in the English language for non-English speakers? It is quite easy to learn, adopt, and use. Like salt, you can sprinkle it everywhere or use it as an adjective, a noun, a verb, an interjection, or an adverb. What other word can do that? "Shit" is not even close!

During my career in consulting, I started allowing myself to drop a few f-bombs here and there after being promoted to director. I ended up being known as the French lady who said "fuck" once in a while. No one thought it was a big deal at that point. I guess my Frenchness was justification or the excuse. "She's French; whatever, let's move on!" To be clear, I was not swearing like a sailor, nor was I being rude, and I would never do it in front of clients. The word would be used for effect to stand my ground and make a point—never toward people.

I then left this formal world of professional services, and I got into the startup world, where all that code of conduct BS went out the door. I have been in meetings with founders yelling at team members they have worked with for more than fifteen years, dropping f-bombs and the rest. It is a completely different world I've had to transition into for the last seven years. Recently, at one of the startups I've been helping, I am a fractional COO, and I am supposed to represent HR. But in a team meeting, the founder made a joke, calling me a bitch. I naturally replied, "What's next? You're going to call me the 'C-word'?" I caught myself, reminding everybody that I was, at that moment, representing HR. Everybody on the call was laughing, but I was thinking, *We will never be able to have a proper HR representative. We'd be completely screwed with this kind of behavior.* In addition to that, apparently, I was loud enough that my husband had to come out of his office and tell me to quiet down as his team on Zoom had heard me and were wondering what was happening. Without the context, I guess they were a bit shocked.

Maybe cursing should be included in the citizenship test. What do you think? I think mastering cursing and its different nuances is a good test of whether you have purposely integrated into the culture. Maybe to be more complete, we also need to include slang words. If you have mastered all of those and you understand the nuances of how people can receive them, then you have made it. This part is harder, especially if you are coming from another country. Without the proper context, you can end up in situations where you make an honest mistake, but some people are straight-up offended.

Different parts of society within the United States also have different standards when it comes to using what is considered foul language. For me, one of my deepest confusions when I first moved here was the N-word. As a foreigner, I understood this word was never to be used, but then I heard it being used in the black community as a term of endearment. And the clueless me was like, wait a minute.

As a white person, I cannot use the word because it is considered bad. But a black person can use the word, and then it is a good word. Again, I didn't have the necessary context to understand that the N-word had been reclaimed by the black community, and that for them, the intent and meaning of the word is changed when it is said by another black person. In France, we have a similar word, which has not been reclaimed, and is considered bad in all communities. Learning curves can be steep when it comes to understanding how to use words in America.

As a foreigner, in addition to learning the language, I also had to navigate these cultural or community differences and try not to offend anyone with my lack of knowledge. Despite the rich and long history of wars in Europe, and each country having its own sensitivities, language still feels more loaded in the United States than it does back in Europe. Why? Perhaps because the differences and animosities in Europe have been going on for centuries and people have only been left to laugh and cry about it. My husband and I do it at home: He is English; I am French; and our countries have been at war for centuries, which makes it for a very lively household. He reminds me time and again about France surrendering in 1941 or the English winning this or that battle. What can we say? The roast beef against the frogs!

Americans also seem to curse more as they get upset. It seems to flow more smoothly on the tongue than in France. Perfect example: "Are you fucking kidding me?" The emotions conveyed by that sentence can range from joy to anger. It's as if by using this word Americans show their emotions through language. Instead of using your hands like those of us in Latin European countries, you use curses to communicate how you feel. It is freaking amazing. I am freaking pissed! Are you fucking kidding me?

Cursing carries a lot of weight in America, too. People take notice if you curse, especially if you say "fuck," and they get offended in some cases. It's not the same in France, where if someone says *"putain de merde,"* the other person will be thinking, *All right bitch, I'll leave you alone and move on.* Early in my career, I managed to offend some of my clients by mistakenly saying, "This is fucking stupid," in a client meeting. It wasn't my proudest moment. It just came out. I was young and passionate, and obviously, having a filter didn't register with me at the time. But I couldn't understand why someone got offended because my comment was not directed at a specific person but at the process that was being put in place. My young French side just didn't get it. I wouldn't do it again—I think I have learned by now—but it was interesting that my using a curse when talking about the process could be perceived as an offense to someone. At times, I have felt that Americans are more emotional than French people or maybe more sensitive—thinner-skinned somehow. Maybe Americans need to be more direct, which I think helps you develop a thicker skin. You learn to take things less personally!

CHAPTER 19

Patriots on the Field

My first experience with the importance Americans put on sports was with college football. During my first quarter at UW, I got invited to join my American boyfriend and his friends to attend the Apple Cup, which is the big rivalry game between UW and Washington State University. That particular year, the game was held in Pullman, Washington. At this point, I was at least aware that UW had a football team, but I had no clue about the rules of the game. American football is pretty much nonexistent in France, and most of my spectating in the past had been on European football or what you call soccer here. But the boyfriend was a big supporter of sports and college sports, especially since he went to Gonzaga and UW, so I had to learn, right? I got indoctrinated, watched a lot of sports on TV, and even attended a few games—including my first NFL game—within six months of landing. I learned quickly, so not too bad for a French lady. Apart from baseball, the American pastime, which I had to wait until the following spring to figure out, I ended up with a crash course in American sports.

(By the way, when I eventually learned about baseball. I decided it was created for people to get together, catch up over extremely overpriced food and beverages, and check the score occasionally. Seriously, you sit down and chat! Sure, you clap for the team once in a while and stretch your legs in the seventh inning while you sing the song. Two-and-a-half excruciatingly slow hours later, you go home a little poorer. But you had a good time with your friends.)

So, there we were, driving through Washington state to Pullman, a four-hour drive, if I remember correctly (basically halfway through France), to go watch one football game. We got there, and I realized that for our accommodations, we would be crashing in someone's empty house, and there weren't enough rooms or beds to go around. And who ended up sleeping on the floor in a closet? You guessed it, yours truly and her boyfriend. It was weird. But I guess as a poor twenty-two-year-old student, you put up with a lot. The only costs ended up being food and gas. I didn't even pay for the tickets. We dropped our stuff, I got prepped with the boyfriend putting UW stickers on my face, and it was time to head to the game. We walked through the university neighborhood and got into the stadium easily, and I was struck by the size of the stadium and the crowd. It was just packed. Remember, I had just landed with my French frame of reference and didn't know how big college football was, nor did I know about the big rivalry between the teams. We proceeded to our seats, and the marching band came out. I was thinking, *How many kids are in this band?* They were taking up the whole field, playing music, marching, and creating all those shapes. I just kept wondering, *What the heck?* while being impressed at the same time. It definitely was time for pictures on an old-school camera (there were no videos on phones at this time). I had to somehow immortalize the size of this band, the field, and the crowd. I couldn't compare it to anything back home.

Suddenly, the announcer proceeded with, "Ladies and gentlemen, please stand up, remove your hats, and join us in singing the national anthem." Everyone in the stadium stood up, took their hats off, turned toward the flag, and placed their hands on their hearts, almost in unison. All right, now I was *definitely* thinking, *What the heck? What do you mean, the national anthem is going to be played? Is this considered an international game? West versus East Washington? Did I cross a border somewhere on my way here?* I politely followed my boyfriend's lead to be respectful, the least I could do, and I started wondering if this happened at every game. I actually did ask my boyfriend that and he answered, "Yep." To be honest, at this point, I thought it was a joke. I thought they were playing a trick on me because I knew nothing. And guess what? I learned very quickly it was not. After attending more sports games, that moment would quickly come and go. The national anthem again.

This is something that does not happen in France. The national anthem is played mainly for international games of any kind. Not when two teams from the same country play against each other. Isn't that a bit much? I couldn't understand why, but it reinforced my belief in how the United States is such a patriotic country, especially when compared to France. The national pride displayed at that football game wasn't something you'd usually see in France, only during international events such as the World Cup, the Olympics, and so on. American patriotism is, in a way, like a religion. It's as if they've incorporated reminders at every turn: "I know you are at a sporting event, but please do not forget you are in the United States of America. Turn around and don't forget to salute the flag."

It was a 4:00 p.m. game in November right before Thanksgiving in eastern Washington state and this girl was not ready for the cold. We froze our asses off watching the game despite our coats, blankets, and holding each other. What was I thinking? Well, obviously nothing since I didn't know what to expect. UW lost that year, but the highlight for me was that while we were in our seats, the UW mascot Harry the Husky stopped by, and I managed to snap a picture with him carrying me in his arms. Not bad, right? No luck with men, but at least a mascot swept me off my feet! I still have the picture from a disposable camera I had brought with me. It was the proudest moment in my American college career!

This kind of build-up found in American sports culture is something that has always intrigued me. It gets ingrained in kids very early on at school and throughout their school career, even turning into cliques in high school with sports teams and cheerleaders. We do not really have that back home. Of course, children are encouraged to play sports, but it is not part of the school environment. We have PE at school, like in the United States, but outside of that, if a kid is interested in playing a sport or any other extracurricular activity, they have to join a club that is not affiliated with the school. Their parents have to sign them up for it and there are fees. These sports clubs are usually affiliated with the town you live in. They have different age groups, and if kids stick with the same sport, they grow through the age group. Because sports clubs compete against other clubs, not against other schools, there really aren't big school rivalries based on sports. There are still rivalries but for other reasons. If you participate in sports clubs, practices and games take place outside of school hours. In this way, school sports are not the path to becoming a professional athlete in France; clubs are. We also have special programs for some kids who want to join the French national team, during which they both train and get schooled during the day. But those kids don't go to class with the rest of us. They might attend school at the same facilities, but they do not take classes with the rest of the students. They have their own accommodated school schedules.

"If there is no competition between schools in France, where is the fun?" you might ask. Well, there is competition between town clubs, as well as regional and national competitions and championships. Outside of that, at school, kids just become really competitive at sports among friends during PE and pickup games. I would get into trouble in PE when the teacher would put us into teams to play basketball, volleyball, handball, or soccer because I always wanted to play with the boys and not the girls. I always questioned why girls couldn't join the boys' teams. I guess I was already a troublemaker, and my PE teachers would get really annoyed with me, especially in high school. But they would always cave and let me play with the boys. I'd play with them during pickup games anyway, so why should I play solely with the girls at school? Screw this! I think my girl classmates hated me for it, too. I didn't care. I learned to play rough basketball with the boys. Same with volleyball or even soccer. I was not great, but I learned a lot and I think it prepared me for how resilient I would need to be in more male-dominated settings, such as engineering and consulting, for example. I was never intimidated or scared to study and work with men. I could stand up to them—I'd had to do it through sports first—without a care in the world.

Competition changed a little when I went to engineering school in Toulouse. At universities and colleges, we do have school teams, but they are in no way professional or to a level that can be compared with the United States. There is no money in those. You join a team for the pride of representing your school and playing sports. I ended up joining the women's rugby team, very short-lived, and then the volleyball and beach volleyball teams. It was fun, and we would have tournaments against other Toulouse-based schools. It didn't really matter how good I was. Obviously, they expect you to at least know the sport, have played in the last game, and be ready to train. We were not very good, but we had fun.

The sports industry in France is also very different. You have all these professional leagues here—NFL, NBA, MLB, MLS, and NHL. The money they generate is massive. It's a money-making machine, really. It feels almost indecent. You could almost say it has its own economy, with players' salaries, endorsements, ticket sales, merchandise, you name it.

Back home, it is mainly about soccer. This is where the money lies. All the other sports—rugby, basketball, volleyball, hockey, and handball—have leagues, but they are not followed like soccer (maybe with the exception of rugby these days). The players do not make the same amount of money. Some of them have day jobs and play sports. They are really amateur teams, not professional ones, so people mainly follow their town's soccer team—Paris Saint-Germain, Marseille, Lille, Lyon, and so on. People usually grow up supporting one and stick to it in later years. And then you have what I call "special sports events" at which people want to be seen: tennis, Formula 1 racing, horse racing, and golf. Those sports are expensive to practice in France, so fewer people follow them.

For me, it's interesting to run into the kind of hardcore American fans who follow the games every weekend and even travel to encourage their team. They hold season tickets—another thing that only exists for soccer back in France—and some of them have held those tickets for more than fifty years. It was eye-opening to experience this kind of fandom in Texas, going to a University of Texas game. People there even make it a family outing and bring the kids and grandkids. And the money it generates . . . I know UT football even has its own TV channel, the Longhorn Network. I think this qualifies sports as a religion, no? Add to it the fact that some fans idolize the players, and there you have it, folks!

The emotions that sports can generate here are incredible, too. Americans get so invested in the teams they follow: They paint themselves, they go to games half-naked, they shout, they cry, they get upset, they curse. Damn, it's just sports. Nobody died, right? Folks, there is always next time, next game. I sound a bit cynical, but that is the reality.

Another surprising aspect of sports in America is gym culture. I'd heard about it from across the pond but hadn't realized how extensive it was until I experienced it here in America. Once I started living in the United States, I noticed that so many people go to the gym. I decided, okay, time for me to find out what this is all about. I had free access to the UW gym so there I was one day, walking down to the waterfront to make my way into the facility. Holy moly! The gym had more than 20,000 machines, weight areas, huge locker rooms with showers, studios, and two full floors to make you sweat somehow. Add the indoor track and you can pretty much do anything—run, cycle, row, swim, elliptical, step, basically any movement you can think of. So again, this clueless lady was thinking, *Where the heck do I start?* I didn't want to turn into a gym rat. At the same time, I had an epiphany as to why American men looked so buff, especially compared to French guys, who are typically skinnier. Americans were not just born this way. It was the gym! The secret is out!

Growing up in France, there were only a handful of gyms, and going to them was definitely not part of the culture. Only certain people would have memberships. Nowadays, it has changed and even some of my friends go to the gym in Paris. I guess Americans managed to export this, too. I always thought that exercising was about sports or team sports—not willingly going to a facility, doing cardio, and pumping iron! I had to learn about all this. I really got into it after the bad breakup with my first American boyfriend. I couldn't eat and could barely stand being in the house, so one of my really good friends from Sweden took me to work out with him. He put me on a three-day-per-week regimen, working out almost two hours each day. He coached me and taught me how to perform all those lifting exercises. After four months, I ended up in the best shape of my life. I lost weight down to 132 pounds, I felt strong . . . well, the sad part is that I haven't been back down to 132 since. Damn it! The reality is that going to the gym doesn't feel natural to me. I still hate going to the gym or getting started on a workout at home, but I love how I feel afterward. I still would prefer not to do it, or do something else active, such as running, swimming, or playing a team sport.

The longer I have been in America, the less I follow sports. Its novelty has slowly faded over the years. I don't even know what is really going on. It just exists in the periphery. I only watch the Super Bowl for the halftime show these days. I guess this is not one of the things I ended up consistently incorporating into my American diet. Is that a bad thing? Does it make me less assimilated into the culture? Probably. I have also moved a lot, so haven't really had a chance to pick a team— Seattle, San Francisco, New York, Texas. Good teams all around. I just haven't found my itch. And to be frank, that is not where I want to spend my time. I'll let the rest of you cheer on my behalf!

CHAPTER 20

Despite What You've Heard, I'm Really Not That into Wine

Alright, let's clear something up from the start: Not all French people are into wine. And when I say "into it," I mean geeking out about buying and collecting very expensive wines. Like any good French person, I do enjoy wine, and I can be a bit picky about it, but that doesn't mean I am a walking encyclopedia of wine.

One of the reasons I'm not that into wine is that I have a hereditary condition called hepatic porphyria, specifically *porphyria cutanea tarda*. It makes my skin more photosensitive, which can cause chronic blistering and even burns with sun exposure. It's not particularly common and might have been caused by a gene mutation due to the historic inbreeding on my dad's side of the family, who were Russian nobility before 1917. The madness of King George III was most likely caused by a form of hepatic porphyria, and some theories claim vampire myths were inspired by it. My vampire disease prevents me from drinking alcohol and taking a bunch of medicines, including estrogen, progesterone, and penicillin. My brother got lucky and doesn't have the condition, so he has the wonderful joy of being able to get piss drunk!

So, I was raised in a household of light drinkers who mainly enjoyed wine socially while going out or hosting dinner parties. Not the typical French family. My parents knew about good wine but were not connoisseurs, nor did they push some kind of wine education on us, with the exception of how to pick a good bottle at Carrefour and how to discern the right wine to complement what we were having for dinner—white for fish, red for meat, and port for dessert. I do not think that I ever saw my parents opening a bottle or having a drink simply to relax on a school night; it was always associated with a social setting. My parents would drink water or a lot of sparkling water on those nights. We kids would have iced tea or one glass of soda—Coke, Canada Dry, Fanta, or Orangina. We didn't have the same variety of sodas back in France. There was no Mountain Dew and absolutely no Dr Pepper. That was another discovery: Who the heck thought cinnamon in Coke was a good idea? It tastes awful! I have the same feelings about Cherry Coke! I think I managed not to put twenty pounds on when I moved here because we didn't drink a lot of pop back home. I still don't buy or drink it. We do not have any at home. Sparkling water—too much of it, but no pop.

I grew up with no one really teaching me about wine, at least not formally. No one made a big deal about it. We would just buy wine. " Tasting " wine consisted of trying out the full bottle and deciding whether we liked it or not. If we did, we bought it again. If we didn't, we tried something different the next time.

Every time I meet Americans, they are always surprised when I tell them I didn't grow up with a bottle of wine on the table at every meal and I don't know everything about wine. But even French people who grew up with parents drinking wine at every meal don't automatically know about wine. At least, not the way Americans think we do. We learn to understand wine appellations, vineyards, and vintages—not varietals. When people in America first asked me what my favorite red wine was, I would answer Bordeaux and they'd ask what type of *grapes* . . . What do you mean, what type of grapes?! I have no clue. Who cares about the varietal? I had to learn about those over the years so I could have educated conversations about wine with Americans. Funny!

In France, learning about wine is more experiential. A red Bordeaux is full-bodied, and you learn to pair it with heavy meat such as a steak. Now a Chablis or a white Burgundy is good with white fish. You learn by drinking and experimenting with what you should pair together. I never learned what type of grapes were in those wines. Tell me what we are eating, and I'll tell you what I think we should pair it with! Duck is mainly cooked in the Southwest of France, so let's go with a Bordeaux or a Bergerac. If we're eating crêpes, let's have cider from Normandy, not wine.

The concept of just having a glass of wine with no food was foreign to me when I first landed. We didn't have wine bars in Paris when I grew up . . . Why would we? To try it? We'd just have a bottle or two with our meal. That would be "tasting" the wine. If we wanted to have a drink before dinner, we would have a beer, a pastis, or an aperitif, not a glass of wine. Wine is for dinner and digestif to close the night out. It has been part of the fabric of society for a very long time, even playing a part in the French Revolution, with red wine becoming a symbol of liberty, equality, and French republicanism.

In the United States, somehow, it became somewhat of a luxury item. For at least the last thirty years, wine consumption in the United States has been growing, making it the fourth-largest producer of wine behind France, Italy, and Spain, and the largest consumer these days. However, the biggest difference is how expensive wine is here compared to Europe. I still don't understand why a good bottle of wine in the United States has to be in the twenty- to twenty-five dollar range. Even with the exchange rate, that puts a good bottle of wine at eighteen to twenty-one euros, which is way more than I would pay for a very good bottle in France. You can find great wines in the five-to-eight euro range. If you want to drink cheap in the United States, it's beer. Wine and fancy cocktails cost an arm and leg, even during happy hour. And you get a small pour, not a full glass, either.

Even these days I still manage to surprise or offend Americans who are really into wine. Yes, I am French, but I know almost nothing about wine and I've never pretended to—I know just enough to get by. Most recently, I visited a friend in New York whose husband is a big wine guy and always tries to talk to me about wine, even though I have told him several times I am not that kind of gal. I am neither a connoisseur nor a collector. They invited some friends over who brought red wine, and we drank over dinner. I was poured a glass, not having seen the bottle nor having asked about it. At the end of dinner, her husband turned around as they were talking about wine and proceeded to ask me whether I knew what I'd been drinking. I just said no, and he told me it was a Château Lafite 1982, which costs around $1,000. I answered, "Great." He continued, telling me it was a great vintage. And I said, "Of course, it was a great vintage. I am quite aware it was a great year. I was born in 1982. I'm a great vintage, too."

To be honest, personally, the wine was good, but I was not blown away by it. I think wine is very subjective, and we all have different tastes and, therefore, different wine preferences. This friend talked to me in a way that almost felt like I should have been grateful for having been able to try the wine. This is not the relationship I have with wine. Of course, it was great to get the opportunity to try such a bottle of wine, but the luxury and status associated with it doesn't sit right with me. It's so great that the United States has become this major player in the wine industry, and that Americans have learned about all the different types of wine, but how much can someone spend on a bottle of wine? God, please, let's not make it another status item. Let's just enjoy it for what it is: a wonderful beverage that is better paired with good food and good company.

So, what is my favorite wine? I am a bubbles girl. I prefer to have an entire meal with a glass of champagne than either red or white wine. I got it from my grandma, my mom's mom. She would drink champagne with entire meals, and as I got older, it grew on me. Champagne, prosecco, or cava, it's all about the bubbles. I get to celebrate every time I order a drink. And it is good for my weight, with only around ninety calories per glass. I like how light, crisp, fresh, and easy it is on the tongue. I might also be a bit biased since my dad took us to Champagne when I was younger. We took a tour of the Moët & Chandon cellar in Épernay back in 1995. It was so cool as a thirteen-year-old that it became my favorite champagne for a very long time. Now I have a few other favorites!

In terms of reds and whites, I used to like full-bodied Bordeaux but with age, I am more of a pinot and a chardonnay person. I had to eventually figure out what varietals I enjoyed to keep up with my American friends. I also participated in a bunch of tastings in Napa, Sonoma, Russian River Valley, Washington, and Nantucket and, even more recently, made an effort to check out Texas Hill Country wines—or should I say the Disneyland of wines. They still have years of work ahead of them. A handful of wineries are decent; the rest is for the younger generations to have fun, such as Fat Ass Ranch & Winery with their fruit wines! Go check them out! Love the label!

At the end of the day, it is all about trying. All over the world, people are trying to make wine. Even in the United States, you have wine producers in every one of the fifty states. And the fun when you encounter them is to try them and draw your own conclusion. You like it, you don't, or you hate it! It's all very subjective and that's the beauty of it! Making wine is hard; it's more than science, it's art, too. Not everyone can be a winemaker. Making good wine takes talent, like being a perfumer—you need a nose, but you also need a palate.

Funny that I had to come to the United States to learn more about wine. But you still can't take the French out of me. I will always look for a French wine first on a menu and try to select based on the appellation—Bordeaux, Burgundy, Chablis, or Bandol. If I buy a bottle for a special occasion, I will pick a French or Italian bottle. I'll stand in front of the rack and try to balance price and quality because I still cannot justify paying forty dollars for one of those bottles. I *really* can't justify the markup. No way! I love Costco for this. I'll be the first one to take advantage of their prices to secure a few good bottles of French, Italian, or even American wines. And

I always have one of their prosecco bottles in the fridge in case of emergency. I think there is a bit of a misconception that for a wine to be good, it has to be a certain price or even flat-out expensive. I have had expensive wines that I didn't think were that extraordinary. It's about finding what you love, sharing, and enjoying it with your favorite vintage of friends.

EPILOGUE

Joining the Dark Side and Becoming a US Citizen

APRIL 1ST, 2022

April Fool's Day *not*: Today was the day I became a US citizen! It didn't occur to me until standing in line, waiting to get into the oath ceremony room, how big of a deal this was for me and my family's journey. My mom and I were joking this morning while I was driving down that it only took forty years for me to become a US citizen. It was a very special occasion. I only regret that my dad could not be here to witness it. But I hope that if he were still here, he would be proud of me.

He was, of course, the one who set this multigenerational journey in motion, starting when he left Poland for Sweden during the Cold War and secured a job at IBM. He spent twenty years with them, traveling all over the world. During that time, his goal was to immigrate to the United States, wanting to leave Europe and any possibility of another war or living under Communism. He'd fought as a teenager for the Red Army in World War II and his dad, my grandpa, died in a gulag in Siberia in 1957, opposing the Russian communist regime. Dad applied for a green card but was declined. He eventually settled in France, still with IBM.

Fast-forward a few years, after my parents met and married in France, they decided their daughter should be born in the United States. With the help of close American friends, a hospital bed was ready for my birth in Lexington, Kentucky. But as I've mentioned before, no luck, as my mom's doctor refused to let her fly. My first opportunity to become a US citizen—gone!

During my wonderful French upbringing, my mom brought my brother and me to the United States in 1994 for three weeks. That time had such a powerful effect on my teenage mind that I promised myself I would find a way to come study and live in the United States. In my last year of high school, I implored my mom to send me to college in the United States. She tried, but it wasn't in the cards yet again. It would take another five years to make my way to UW in Seattle as a visiting graduate student finishing my master's in aerospace engineering.

Of course, even though the original plan was for me to only stay in the United States for nine months, barely two months into my stay I decided I was going to apply to business school. I took the TOEFL and GMAT but only applied for one MBA program. I couldn't afford any of them, especially the ones closer to home on the East Coast. But my luck finally came through, and UW let me in. With that, nine months turned into three years, and after securing a job at a Big Four firm in San Francisco in 2007, I started a career in the United States.

Staying in America certainly wasn't as easy as coming to America had been. But with securing a job at that Big Four firm came their sponsorship of my first and second H1B visas, as well as my green card. It took me a little more than two years from the time I submitted my first application to receive the physical green card in the mail. But I eventually got it in October 2012. And this was considered quick. Some of my friends from India had it way harder, enduring wait times of ten years or more to get their hands on a green card. And some of them had been in the United States for more than ten, fifteen, or twenty years! I guess being French helped me with that one.

Securing a green card is not really the end of the process, either. To maintain that status, I had to live in the United States at least six months out of the year. If I left, I'd lose it. And I had to renew it every ten years. When that happens, there is always a chance my renewal request will be declined. However, after five years, I became eligible to apply for naturalization. When that time came, I didn't apply. I didn't feel compelled to do it, or like I needed it. I still felt a strong attachment to my home country, and I had doubts about completely embracing my adopted one. I also didn't want to get stuck with having to file US tax returns and pay US taxes every year, especially if I decided to go home for retirement. I simply didn't want to. I know some friends who have been on their green card forever and ever and have no desire to take on citizenship, my husband being one of them.

Last year, my green card came up for renewal, and I thought, *You know what? It's time! It's been forty years since this story of US immigration began, and it is time to close the book and get this done!* At that point, all my earthly possessions and finances were in the United States. If I ever decided to take a job abroad or even retire in Europe, I needed to be able to come back easily. I realized, except for family and friends, I had nothing really left back home in France. America is home now! Funny enough, I also realized it would cost me less money to apply for citizenship than to renew my green card, so I pulled the trigger. I didn't even talk to anyone about it. I just applied and then announced it to everyone: my mom, my brother, my husband, and my friends. Yes, in that order!

I applied on February 8, thinking it was going to take six to eight months or more. That is what they said on the website. So, you can imagine my surprise when I got my appointment papers in the mail two and a half weeks later, asking me to come down to San Antonio for my interview at the end of March. I thought, *Holy crap, I'd better start studying for the test.* I drove down to San Antonio from Austin, aced the test, and answered all their questions, including having to confirm that I hadn't been a Nazi during World War II or a communist during the Cold War. I did challenge the interviewer a bit on that one. I wasn't even born at that time! She apologized and still asked me to give her a yes or no answer. What can I say?

That following Friday, on April Fool's Day, I pledged allegiance and got my certificate of naturalization. I'd like to claim this was the fastest anyone has ever been naturalized in this country. Ha! I do not know if it was because of COVID or if they just looked at all the pictures and fingerprints they had of me entering the country over the years, the fact that I paid my taxes religiously every year, or that I had no criminal record. In any case, they must've thought, *Fine, let's get this fool in and charge her more taxes.* And that is how I joined the Dark Side.

After almost twenty years, my friends back in France, who've been referring to me as "the American," can now officially call me an American. And my friends here in the United States, who always referred to me as French, cannot do so any longer. I am French American. I guess I have two citizenships, so they can just call me whatever they want!

I am humbled to have finally become an American citizen. I am thankful for all this country has brought me: knowledge, career, friends, and family. I look forward to giving back. First stop: voter registration! I guess I cannot claim innocence in the US political process any longer. The most recent 2024 presidential election was the first time I was able to fully participate in the process and make my voice heard. Now that they have let me in, I am obliged to do my civic duty. I guess paying my taxes for the last twenty years has paid off. Now that I am in, I am all in!

It's been a journey for sure, but one I'm happy to have undertaken. Back when I was standing at the Paris airport, finally leaving for the United States, my dad whispered in my ear, "Never come back!" Well, I didn't, and I hope you are proud!

Acknowledgments

I extend my heartfelt gratitude to all those whose support, encouragement, and laughter have made this book possible.

To my family, for their unwavering belief in my dreams and their endless love. Thank you for always being my anchor and my biggest fans. Special thanks to my dad for encouraging me to never return, and my partner for putting up with my antics.

To my friends and work colleagues, both old and new, who have shared my adventures and provided inspiration with their own stories, and whose excitement for the idea behind this book and impatience for its release gave me the kick in the butt I needed to get it done!

A special thank you to the incredible people I've met along the way. Some of them made it into the book, which added layers of hilarity to these pages. You are the reason why I am still here, so thank you!

To my editors, whose keen ears, eyes, and thoughtful suggestions have shaped this memoir into its best form. Thank you for helping me make this book a reality!

To the team at the publishing house for their dedication and enthusiasm in bringing *French Landing* to life.

And to the readers, thank you for embarking on this comedic escapade with me. May the tales of culture clashes, dating disasters, and American oddities bring a smile to your face and warmth to your heart.

About the Author

ELISABETH BYKOFF was born in Nice, France, over forty-two years ago and currently holds both American and French citizenship.

Elisabeth arrived in the United States twenty years ago and graduated with two master's—one in aerospace engineering from l'École Nationale de l'Aviation Civile and the other in business administration from the University of Washington. She still wonders how she managed to stay at school for so long.

Formerly a business consultant, a tech startup executive, a skydiver, and a motorcycle rider, Bykoff has now decided to start on her own journey as a tech founder.

She loves the silver screen and devours audiovisual content. An avid traveler, she has visited more than fifty countries and can't wait to set foot on the one continent she hasn't visited yet: Antarctica. She even got married in Belize!

Bykoff has had to open her emergency parachute before, she had to evacuate a plane once, and she even survived dating in America.

Now, she shares her home in Texas with her husband, two extraordinary mutts, and a collection of books.